Praise for U

"This book helps me understand the impact of Urban Trauma on conditions in my city that my administration works to ameliorate. Dr. Akbar's poignant stories and insight into negative, often disruptive behaviors of children—and adults—living with multigenerational trauma provides a foundation for understanding these problems and provides tools to address these complex limiting behaviors."

-Toni Harp, Mayor, New Haven, Connecticut

"Dr. Akbar pokes her finger deep into the painful pulse of today's urban communities—clearly outlining behaviors and characteristics that have proven efficacious for some but a detriment to many others. As the mother of two black boys, *Urban Trauma* is a cultural masterpiece connecting the dots of history and the burden of proof that deals directly with what has been, what is, and what is to come."

-Staci L. Hallmon, Vice President,
Essence Communications

"*Urban Trauma* defines a harrowing space in America's subconscious of things unsaid, but certainly understood by so many. With both eloquence and unapologetic candor, Dr. Akbar excavates the root causes of racism and the ensuing broken social paradigms through which our youth must navigate. This work is long overdue."

-James R. Nowlin, J.D., Best-selling author of
The Purposeful Millionaire, *and CEO of Excel Global Partners*

"Understanding the complex experience of the African diaspora requires consideration of the impact of Urban Trauma on their health and mental health outcomes. Dr. Akbar, in her seminal work, is challenging the field of psychology and practitioners, specifically, to integrate the experiences of groups whose voices and experiences have continued to be muted as we work to heal the ills that they experience. Important, timely, and required!"

-Derrick M. Gordon, PhD, Associate Professor of Psychiatry (Psychology Section) Division of Prevention & Community Research Yale University School of Medicine Director of Research, Policy & Program on Male Development, The Consultation Center at Yale

"*Urban Trauma* is a must read for clinicians and all professionals working within and across the color-line. Dr. Akbar provides the reader with a unique and comprehensive view of trauma; one that expands our understanding and deepens our work with children, adolescents, adults, and families that have lived and adapted to traumatic experiences. We are compelled as clinicians, physicians, and clergy to utilize this knowledge in our efforts to heal the invisible wounds of our communities."

-Dr. Brett S. Rayford, Director of Program Development, Albert J. Solnit Children Center, A program of the CT Department of Children and Families

"*Urban Trauma* is a powerful and thoughtful piece on racism and the impact it has on Black communities. Dr. Akbar gives a detailed script for clinical and social practitioners as well as community advocates who are in the daily trenches fighting for social change and equality."

-Shahid Abdul-Karim, New Haven Register Community Engagement Editor

"As a pastor serving an urban congregation for the last 32 years I have seen the effects of racism and the trauma it produces. Dr. Akbar illuminates these issues from a fresh perspective and *Urban Trauma* represents a teaching tool that everyone who works in communities affected by these issues should read."

-Rev. Dr. Boise Kimber, Sr. Pastor of
The First Calvary Baptist Church,
New Haven, Connecticut

"This book serves as an invaluable resource to urban America. My job as a law-enforcement professional demands that I ensure that institutional racism has as little effect on my organization as possible. However, more importantly, as a father, it's imperative that each of my sons is empowered to take charge of their destinies, not simply by being taught how to navigate the turbulent waters which are continually stirred up by institutional racism, but to use those waters to guide them into a future where they have control over their destinies. Dr. Akbar's book is one such tool which I'm sure will help them get there."

-Anthony Campbell, Chief of Police,
New Haven Police Department

"Dr. Akbar gives a targeted view of the trauma that is pervasive and plagues sectors of the Black community. As an educator, I am keenly aware of the historical and familial nuances that pattern the lives of our children. However, as educators, we grapple with appropriate identification of needs and may misidentify students with a disability, when in reality the needs are appropriate social/emotional supports and tools to allow for success. Educators will be able to use this book as a resource to connect several underlying emotional pathways for the students they serve. *Urban Trauma* is a tool for discovery and action."

-Melanie T.B. Mandisodza, M. Ed.
Director of Student Support Services,
Homewood School District 153—suburb of Chicago

"In this current political climate, Dr. Akbar has brilliantly reminded us of the day-to-day challenges that our Black urban youth face and about the complexities of institutionalized racism that continues to plague us. She provides an accessible framework for any trained education professional working with students in academic settings."

-Dr. Michell Tollinchi-Michel, PhD,
Higher Education Professional

URBAN TRAUMA

URBAN TRAUMA

A Legacy of Racism

Maysa Akbar, PhD, ABPP

PUBLISH YOUR PURPOSE PRESS

For permission requests, write to the publisher, addressed "Attention: Permissions Coordinator," at the address below.

Publish Your Purpose Press
141 Weston Street, #155
Hartford, CT 06141

The opinions expressed by the Author are not necessarily those held by Publish Your Purpose Press.

Ordering Information: Quantity sales and special discounts are available on quantity purchases by corporations, associations, and others. For details, contact the publisher at the address above.

Edited by: Heather B. Habelka
Cover design by: Graphixa

Printed in the United States of America.

ISBN: 978-1-946384-24-9 (print)
ISBN: 978-1-946384-17-1 (ebook)
Library of Congress Control Number: 2017950797

First edition, September 2017

Publish Your Purpose Press works with authors, and aspiring authors, who have a story to tell and a brand to build. Do you have a book idea you would like us to consider publishing? Please visit PublishYourPurposePress.com for more information

8/2018

Rahsaan, Kyoshi & Kalilah—my everything
To all Pan-Africans, claim your rightful place in this world
and declare triumph.

ACKNOWLEDGMENTS

There are so many people who deserve acknowledgment. In an unconventional gesture I want to thank all of those who have knowingly or unconsciously created relationship challenges, made things uncomfortable for me, and over complicated simple situations. Each of these instances became training opportunities to get stronger, tougher, wiser, and ultimately braver. I have persevered through every single challenge and will continue to be a trailblazer because of you! A very dear friend and colleague, Dr. Brett Rayford once told me, "While many people are obstacle creators, I am an obstacle eliminator." Those words ring true daily.

I have to thank my mother, who often has no idea what I do for a living or the impact that I make daily on the lives of people, but whose innocence makes me smile. Especially, when she questions why I come home so late or why I get so many awards. I also have to thank my father who taught me about work ethic, imparted the importance of education, and placed me in situations where I mastered overcoming struggle. While we never reconciled our relationship, I hope he knows that I have long forgiven him and that I am at peace. Hats off to those who had a hand in raising me: my grandparents, my aunts, and cousins—it really does take a village. Now as a mom and wife I completely understand what it takes to raise a child, especially one that is not your own. To Gail and Roger Mahabirsingh, my role models, who taught me what a loving marriage and parenting relationship should look like. You've been instrumental in setting us on the path to raising our children right. To my in-laws Beverly Richards, Madeline Gulston, and Madeline Ford, you have all been rock solid for the last twenty years. To the Akbar clan, I love each and every one of you. Ngozi, thank you for being such an amazing sister. Nathifa, thank you for your creativity and supporting this book launch. Your talent knows no bounds.

To my illustrious sorority, Delta Sigma Theta, Inc., and the founders who graciously paved the way. Most importantly, my line sisters who have been there through life's ups and downs. My Jack and Jill family, especially Toni Ligon and Thais Moore, I am so appreciative that you are both a second mom to Kalilah. Karaine Holness, Robyn Porter, Babz Rawls Ivy and Sara Lulo—all distinguished women of intelligence, grace, and influence.

To my soul sister, Dr. Michell Tollinchi-Michel, what can I say… words cannot describe my gratitude for your unwavering commitment to me, my family, and my personal growth throughout the years… you are truly my ride or die. To my lifelong sister friends, LaNae Shelton and Elsa Gaverlidou—you have influenced my life in so many ways. Super couples Theron and Kim Grant and Jose and Carol Ruiz my gratitude for endless years of laughter, bickering tirades, and most importantly your abundance of love. You have taught me that there is beauty in our imperfections. My goddaughters Mia Asenjo and Danielle Nelson, your generation brings new possibilities and hope.

I also want to acknowledge those who created a space around me, and gave me the opportunity to write this book. Kyisha Velazquez, a force to be reckoned with, thank you for your encouragement and undeniable support. Dr. Kaity Hutchinson, you are a fortress. I am very appreciative of your analytical eye and all the research support, along with Mariyah Charlton. To Jessica Mommens and the staff at Integrated Wellness Group, your work—our work—is what made this book possible. Continue to strive beyond your wildest expectations.

Rahsaan Akbar, my husband of twenty years: You are my inspiration and my motivation. Your quiet strength shakes the earth. Growing up into adulthood with you has been an extraordinary ride. I would have it no other way. Thank you for taking care of our family and our children the way that you do. To my son Yoshi, you brought my book cover to life! Thank you for being my counselor, the yin to my yang, and my emotional healer. My daughter Kalilah, the brains of the operation and our baby genius. My love for you is so profound. I appreciate your strength, sobering feedback, and courage. You keep me young. All three of you challenge me daily to create the best version of me, over and over.

It would be impossible for me to end without acknowledging the many wonderful Black and Brown people that I have met throughout the years as they searched for their emotional wellness. You have been the real teachers, showing me the struggles we face as a people, but also how to persevere and ultimately reconcile our duplicity.

We are going to emancipate ourselves from mental slavery because whilst others might free the body, none but ourselves can free the mind. Mind is your only ruler, sovereign. The man who is not able to develop and use his mind is bound to be the slave of the other man who uses his mind; use your intelligence to work out the real things of life. The time you waste in levity, in non-essentials, if you use it properly you will be able to guarantee your posterity a condition better than you inherited from your forefathers.

—Marcus Garvey, leader in the Black Nationalist Movement

Contents

A Note from the Author

Our history predicates the common ancestral struggle that exists in the Black community; Black history is shared by all of us. However, as you read the book take note that not all Black people have Urban Trauma, our individual situations are different and unique.

FOREWORD

Two months ago I had a nice apartment in Chicago. I had a good job. I had a son. When something happened to the Negroes in the South I said, "That's their business, not mine." Now I know how wrong I was. The murder of my son has shown me that what happens to any of us, anywhere in the world, had better be the business of us all.—MAMIE TILL, 1955

I have known Maysa for over nineteen years. When I first met her, she was a new wife and mother, working with youth in one of the most troubled urban sections of St. Louis, Missouri. I could see that she was a fiery counselor committed to assuring that the young people she served received high quality culturally competent care and had access to the resources that they would need to succeed. She was acutely aware of the discrimination and marginalization young Black and Brown people faced and the shortcomings of the system that served them. For reasons that she did not share, she was laser focused on earning a doctorate to successfully address the issues that she identified in the community, from a position of knowledge and expertise. When we met, I was focused on racial identity development research, of which she showed a great deal of interest. The strength of her Black identity was apparent; it was clear she spent considerable time understanding herself, her African roots, and based on this, becoming a lifelong advocate for the community she served.

I realize now how little I knew about Maysa the woman, her

personal history, development, struggles, and efforts to overcome the life that many urban children faced. I did not know, and she did not immediately reveal that she often saw herself in them. She knows more than most in the service professions what it would take for them to overcome the challenges that they faced, but she also knew that they had the strength and the talent to succeed rather than merely survive. She approached me to provide feedback on her application to clinical psychology programs, which she really did not need. My comments were a security blanket, because (as I would come to understand was habit) Maysa had done her homework and had the situation well in hand.

It would take years as her mentor and then her friend for me to fully comprehend who this woman was and is. But, I immediately realized that she was a rare talent—clinically and in her ability to understand and connect to individuals who are in emotional pain and be responsive to community needs. Over the years, I would witness her determination, initiative, and strength as she faced each new challenge. Slowly, she would share her story and I would come to understand the depth of some of her pain, anxiety, and many insecurities, while admiring her resilience. I did not realize how her experiences would come full circle to inform her latest contribution to the profession in the form of her first book, *Urban Trauma*.

I watched as Maysa entered her doctoral program and completed her dissertation, moving on to successfully complete her pre- and post-doctoral internship. I have cheered and experienced a great deal of pride watching her professional development. She became the first—and remains the only—woman of color in Connecticut to achieve certification from the American Board of Professional Psychology through the examination and certification demonstrating competence in professional psychology (considered by many an elite level of study in Psychology). Maysa has systemically built a clinical practice that is innovative and provides the same high quality care that has been rooted since the beginning of her career. Dr. Akbar and her team deliver evidence-based mental health services in a culturally sensitive manner, mostly to communities that need it the most. Just as she intended, she has been and is able to respond to client and community needs in a way that overcomes the mental health concerns, mistrust, and fear of stigma that decades of social and economic discrimination, poverty and deprivation, as well as marginalization can produce. She has been able to do all of this while being a wife, raising two beautiful children, and becoming a leader in her community. Maysa is able to do what she does because of her passion for people, particularly communities of color and the unwavering desire to right a grievous wrong. It is this understanding and sensitivity that *Urban Trauma* outlines and makes real for the reader.

Maysa and I discussed this book about four years ago. On a recent trip to New England, just over a year ago, I stopped in to visit her. She brought up the idea of the book again. We discussed various components of the idea with the notion of Urban Trauma being a central issue. I noted that the term really did not appear in the existing clinical literature and that traditional trauma researchers and clinicians might balk at this new terminology. She noted my feedback, but wanted to push the norm, and innovate in this area: something that Maysa does often! We discussed similar concepts and strategies for explaining this idea. Her ability to integrate psychology into a genuine topic that affects urban communities is exceptional; add to that examples that are peppered with her own life experiences, her substantial clinical experience and expertise, and that of others in her practice, as well as her professional colleagues. As I realized that she was discussing these issues with others, it became apparent to me that Dr. Akbar had once again decided that there was an issue to be addressed, and if no one else was there to tackle it, she would fearlessly take it on.

I gave her my opinions on how she should approach the book, strategies for disciplining herself so that she could get the writing done. I see some of my advice, but in usual fashion, there is so much more than I considered. *Urban Trauma* is divided into three logical sections. The first sections examine life in the Black community, moving the reader from historic to current social, political, and economic factors that lead to trauma exposures. These sections discuss the relevant issue *without* the automatic assumption that there is something wrong with Black people and the Black community. Instead, they suggest that we begin with the sensitizing question of what experiences might contribute to the distress and difficulty that can be observed while coping. The second part defines Urban Trauma within the context of historic discrimination and its economic consequence, poverty, as well as the other sequelae that impact, in particular, Black socio-emotional well-being. The book ends with a focus on the factors that drive our resiliency as a community. What makes this book special is the way the author opens up and shares her own experience with Urban Trauma. Maysa's willingness to share assists professional and lay members of the community to move past the stigma of mental illness, the social norms that require women to be long suffering, and men to be so macho that none of us can see the other's pain. This book takes the reader through a journey with the hope of finding a safe place to heal. The book also forces each of us to take responsibility for asking, "What happened to you?" and being willing to listen. Lastly, it provides a call to action, challenging readers to focus on one person, one agenda, one movement that will uplift our people, especially those that have been left behind.

Perhaps that was the problem in my early relationship with Maysa. I didn't know her story, but then again, I never asked. This is a book as much about the community that we create together, as it is about mental health and well-being. I began this foreword with what is probably the most famous quote from Mamie Till because everything in this book hearkens back to her words. What happens in Black communities is the business of us all, AND healing from what happens is also the business of us all.

—Dr. Vetta Thompson, PhD
Professor, Brown School, Washington University in St. Louis, MO
Licensed Psychologist

PREFACE

Being Black in America has very little to do with skin color. To be Black means that your heart, your soul, your mind, and your body are where the dispossessed are.—JAMES H. CONE

I coined the term Urban Trauma out of a profound sense of personal—and academic—responsibility. First, to help urban communities understand that the psychological damage they continue to endure dates back generations. Second, to help mental health professionals, educators, non-profit and community leaders better understand the urban communities they serve.

It is commonplace for some outsiders to look down at the Black community and wonder why economic and social disparities still exist when they, like all others, "have been given the opportunity to grab themselves by the boot straps and do better." Many Black folks, despite facing pretty severe adversity, have done better. They have broken the cycle of poverty, crime, abuse, drugs, gang violence, and incarceration. They have been able to follow a path that was either paved by the blood of their ancestors or they themselves created, through their own blood, sweat, and tears.

It is important to view history as part of a complex algorithm, that defines the current status of Black communities all over this country. An important factor that is often left out of the calculation, is the role of Urban Trauma. It is often easier to blame the misfortune of Black communities on bad parenting, lack of education, poor work ethic, motivational lows, and a host of other reasons rather than to consider the role of intergenerational Urban Trauma. Add to this a layer of stigma associated with mental health and you have a perfect combination of a group of people who live in pain and who suffer (sometimes silently, sometimes not so silently) but never get the appropriate treatment. Lack of therapeutic support, clinicians who are culturally competent, and access to appropriate treatment enables the continuation of intergenerational transmittal of racial trauma.

There are so many mental health and direct service "allies" who talk from a distance about the Black community and what we need. The reality is that there are few of those who would go into the 'hood with a kid or adult, spend time getting to know them, and understand their struggle firsthand. In fact, most who make it to the management level rarely leave the comfort of their offices. But you can't become an expert in Urban Trauma if you sit in an office all day and never talk, touch, or connect with the very people whose struggle has become the pipeline for funding your organization. Regardless of my degrees, awards, and recognition in my field, I talk to a large majority of the young people we serve at my New Haven, Connecticut-based practice, Integrated Wellness Group. I go to court, I go to school meetings, and I talk to their parents to help them become better parents despite their circumstances. I plant seeds of hope expecting nothing in return. I do so because I have a genuine love for the Black community and I want to see us rise beyond the emotional pain and psychological bondage of Urban Trauma.

For years, I struggled with how to really help the most disenfranchised people in our communities. Unlike other "experts" in the field, I did not come into the work believing that I knew how to solve all the problems or with the desire to become anyone's savior—a complex many mental health providers contend with. Instead, drawing from the same way I approach everything in my life, I became a student and focused on learning from the community I serve and have become a part of.

Many Black folks who live in urban impoverished communities see no way out of their current situation and either try to survive or reach a place of hopelessness and despair. But I believe my responsibility as a psychologist who has been in the field for over fifteen years is to bring the concept of Urban Trauma to the table. I completed a Master's Degree at Florida A&M University (FAMU), a Historical Black College or University (HBCU), and in my opinion the mecca for the most dynamic Black psychologists in this country. It was important for me to learn about community work before I immersed myself in the world of individual counseling. During my time at FAMU, I was challenged to think about mental health beyond the scope of treatment modalities by beginning to understand the role of race in human behavior. I was first intrigued by identity development, and more specifically racial identity. Researching racial identity was interesting on many levels because I myself was on a journey to discover my own. It was a time in my life where I was morphing into being comfortable in my own skin despite the labels that society placed on me, and what people assumed based on the color of my skin and my country of origin.

As an immigrant from the Dominican Republic (DR), I was told from the moment I arrived in this country that I am "Hispanic." I really didn't know what this meant since in the DR, as in most Caribbean islands, you do not identify by ethnic categories. Instead you identify with your nationality. To me I was Dominican, plain and simple. That narrative changed significantly for me once I came to this country. As an undergrad I began to read history books, take African and Caribbean Studies classes, and began to understand that the label of "Hispanic" (a political label rather than a racial category) did not connect me to my people, my ancestors. I learned that in the seventeenth century, when the Dominican Republic and Haiti were one island (Hispaniola) they fought and won against slavery—the first country to abolish slavery in the Western Hemisphere. I began to develop great pride for my African roots and an understanding that despite my biracial skin complexion, I come from a line of African warriors, fighters, and abolitionists. I rejected labels that made me feel inferior and made an intentional decision not to identify with my European ancestry—those whom I considered the catalyst to my/our oppression. Today in the U.S. I am classified ethnically as Latina—a misclassification in my opinion; since racially I identify as Black. This makes all the sense in the world to me as there are 7.8 million Blacks in the Dominican Republic (ranked fourth for countries with the highest Black populations outside of Africa, and higher than both Jamaica and Trinidad, DR's neighboring West Indian islands).

The maturity of my racial identity and my expanded awareness of my cultural roots allows me to stand firm in my Pan-Africanism (the worldwide intellectual movement that aims to encourage and strengthen bonds of solidarity between all people of African descent). As a Dominican woman, whose island is located in the West Indies and was populated by hundreds of thousands of enslaved Africans who fought and won freedom from slavery, I am completely unapologetic about my claim to my African roots and to my Blackness. With that said, I recognize two things: My light complexion allows me to move swiftly between two worlds that are more divided than they are united. My light complexion also allows me a subset of privileges that my dark-skinned brothers and sisters do not have, because they cannot hide their Blackness or "pass" like I am able to do upon first sight. I recognize this, I have learned to accept it, and in the same breath, I will never stop fighting for our freedom from oppression and discrimination, and for the ultimate attainment of our mental and emotional healing.

Throughout the book you will see that I use Black as the descriptor. Why Black instead of African American? We could argue that Black is a color and does not adequately represent the people in the community that I reference throughout this book. But I am not interested in arguing that point. I am interested in inclusivity of all people of color who identify with their African heritage, but may not feel the patriotism connected to being American. I wanted to include folks from the Caribbean, Central and South America, Europe, Africa, and throughout the world. People who feel restricted by the term African American, but feel included when categorized as Black. In Africa if you were to say you were African American they would ask what country? What tribe? What does it really mean to be African (the continent with 54 independent countries) American? I wanted to be intentional in my semantics, and careful in my choice around selecting Black, a term which is inherently inclusive of any Black person from anywhere in the world who lives in the U.S. That includes me.

My passion for finding the truth did not stop as an undergraduate. I quickly understood that in order to survive and progress I needed to continue down a path of higher education, where I would see fewer people who looked like me and where I would be considered radical in my thinking. I left Tallahassee, Florida, to purse a PhD at St. Louis University (SLU), a far cry from Brooklyn, New York, where I grew up.

Completing my degree at SLU was no easy task, but I found a wonderful mentor who nurtured my spirit and supported my work, Dr. Vetta Sanders Thompson. She got me through the most difficult challenges and believed in me even when I lost sight of believing in myself. I saw moments of devastating failure and was even told by one professor that I did not have the pedigree to be a psychologist. He was right, I did not have the traditional pedigree that he was used to seeing in this very elite program. But I had an unwavering determination that even he could not diminish.

As life would have it, this young girl who lived a transient lifestyle as an adolescent in the streets of New York, ended up getting placed at the Yale School of Medicine, Child Study Center. I took it all in. I did not waste a single minute of my time at Yale. I learned from the best to become the best. I learned to be an innovator, a trailblazer, and a scholar. I took all of my life's learning, plus my professional experiences and became a resident expert in the psychology of race. I have spent eleven years studying this very topic, writing a thesis, and defending a dissertation that mirrored my learning. Now fifteen years after completing my postdoc I have worked with the most fascinating people of color, day in and day out, with each contact enhancing my understanding of the mental state of our communities. Decades of study and research have helped me define and explain Urban Trauma; identify how the history of racial trauma has brought us to this point; and how to innovate solutions for healing, reconciling with the past, and ultimately achieving emotional emancipation.

In this book we will look at the historical facts that illustrate specifically how Urban Trauma has evolved in the Black community, illuminating how the past predicts the future. I will help you connect the dots through historical events, basic biology, and the psychological conditions that plague Black communities. Because Urban Trauma does not have symptoms, but instead has characteristics, I will take you through a thoughtful journey on how to understand the framework of Urban Trauma and incorporate it into your work.

If we continue to deny that Urban Trauma is a real and pervasive issue in our communities, then we deny ourselves the possibility of healing and finally breaking a cycle that has plagued our people for way too long.

PART I

Section One: Trauma in Black History

My Urban Trauma

In my mind, the situation in my house was normal. As a child, I did not understand that my circumstances were different from other children. As in many Dominican families, my father was the head of the house, made all the decisions, and was not to be questioned—his word was law. I never had a good relationship with my father growing up. He was very strict and often extremely harsh and abrasive. He often became very irritable, even over minor things. His frustration toward my mother and me was made very clear. In my eyes, he made my mother out to be someone who was of inferior intellect, was overly driven by emotions, lacked logic, and had no common sense. Back then, my mother was a very passive and meek woman. On the outside, all the negative things my father said about my mother seemed pretty true to me. I observed her being obedient to him, worked in a low-skilled factory job, and usually had very few opinions about our home environment. I, on the other hand, was very "spirited." I questioned things and I pushed the envelope even during times when it was probably better for me to remain quiet. For these reasons, I grew to despise my mother's weakness, and vowed to never be like her. The anger toward my father grew as he became more punitive, as did the resentment toward my mother for not protecting me from the monster that I called Dad.

There was this one instance that is forever etched in my memory. I was probably around ten years old, when a group of my cousins who lived in a nearby neighborhood in Queens, New York, stopped by our house to say hello. It was a beautiful summer day. We were living in South Ozone Park at the time. They rang the doorbell repeatedly, but playfully as did many young kids during that time when they wanted a friend to come outside and play. I was hesitant to answer because just a few hours before, my father left to run several errands. My mother worked in a factory so she was gone most of the day. I stayed in the house alone quite a bit from a very young age. As they stood outside the front door, I contemplated whether I would answer the door or not. I thought to myself, what harm would it do? My father had left explicit instructions not to open the door for anyone. But again, I thought, these are my cousins. That has to be different. As an alternative solution, I decided that instead of letting them in, I would sit with them outside on our front stoop. We can talk, laugh, and have a good time without them actually coming into the house. I was proud that I had made this great decision all on my own, as I did not want to upset either my father or my cousins. I proceeded to open the door and sat outside with my cousins for about an hour before my father came home. We played hopscotch, made games from scratch paper, talked about boys we liked, and laughed about how they had tortured me the previous weekend by making me watch both *Friday the 13th* and the Freddy Krueger horror movie back to back (I didn't really think it was very funny but I went along with it). I was really happy, at that moment, mostly because I was not alone. Relationships were so important to me. I spent so much time alone in the house that any human contact was so very appreciated.

When my father arrived, he seemed okay. He did not yell—he

was often pretty explosive. So I expected that if I did something wrong he would start fussing at me right away in front of my cousins without a single care. As he passed us on the front steps he ordered me to come into the hallway that led to the apartment of the two-family house. When I walked into the corridor, he had a belt in his hand and began to beat me with the buckle of that belt. He hit me so hard I fell to the ground, crying, in a state of shock. I tried to protect myself by lifting my arm up. My cousins heard the screams, they busted into the corridor and my father, exasperated, told them, "This is what happens when you open the door to strangers." I howled that they were "not strangers; they are family," at which point the physical assault became even more aggressive. My cousins screamed for him to stop and my father eventually threw them out of the house.

As I lay there limp, I cried and cried and cried. I felt weak and unsafe. The realization that I had no one to protect me sunk in. I was afraid and confused. I did not have the strength to get up. Shortly after, he dragged me further inside the house and told me to go take a bath. This was a common practice after he beat me. The wounds would sting more when you immersed them in warm water, especially if you have broken skin. At this point, I had no choice but to do what he told me. It was painful; I felt so alone. He made me sit in the bath for what felt like hours. I remember my skin pruning.

When I was finally released, I thought I would be able to go into my own space to deal with the pain of my wounds and to grieve. I don't know if my embarrassment was worse than the physical pain, but both were equally devastating. I was mad at myself for making such a stupid decision—he did after all say not to open the door to anyone. I beat myself up mentally, over and over, contemplating all the reasons why I was not good enough. Shortly after putting some clothes on, the physical abuse continued. Now it was time for me to kneel and think about what I did. This was considered a longer-term punishment for my misbehavior. The beating was not enough of a punishment, so kneeling on bottle caps was the next phase. I kneeled there in pain until my mother arrived home from work. I just looked at her, tears rolling from my eyes, my knees bruised, my body aching, and my heart crushed to a million pieces. Anger and despair flooded me, as this was one of many beatings I received. And in my heart, I knew it would not be the last.

While I do not recall exactly how I got out of the kneeling position and removed the bottle caps that were stuck to my knees, I do remember my mother cleaning my wounds and crying as she did it. It was such a painful moment for us both. No real words were spoken then. The only thing remaining was a specter of abuse, which left its devastating mark on the victims it devoured.

From Trauma to PTSD

There are times when a person experiencing trauma feels like they are having an out-of-body experience because reality is often too painful to accept. Traumatic events come in many different forms. Sometimes it is through abuse (physical, sexual, verbal, emotional, and/or psychological), sometimes it happens through what you witness, such as violence in your community, extreme poverty, or a crime committed against you or someone you love.

Trauma can be subjective to the person experiencing the event because we all have different breaking points for stress in our lives. What I consider stressful may not be stressful to you at all. And while this book is not meant to be used as a diagnostic tool, it is meant to help you raise your level of understanding of Urban Trauma. You can then provide a safe space for those who have

Urban Trauma: in your life, in your work, or in your community, and evaluate their past by exploring the possibility that they may have encountered multiple traumatic events in their life. You will consider the role of ancestral racial trauma—this builds trust, opens up the opportunity to work together on a deeper level, and encourages working through past or present trauma.

I am positive that until I got into the field of psychology I never realized, or wanted to accept, that I myself had experienced Urban Trauma. I just had a father with a bad temper and old school ways of dealing with misbehavior who beat me when I deserved it. That was my script and I stuck to it. It helped me survive my situation. Perhaps I did not realize it because, from my point of view, it never affected the way I functioned on the outside. But on the inside, I was always operating in survival mode. I developed coping mechanisms and nothing and no one could ever get in the way of what I needed or wanted.

"People like me are not traumatized!"

At least that is what I told myself. But the reality is that the same thing that drove me to create a survival mode to begin with was the very thing that fueled me to survive. When you live in stressful situations, all you think about is a way out, a way to persist, and a way to beat the odds. You do not have the luxury to stop and think about why you behave the way you do.

Eventually I learned that my childhood was not as normal as I thought it was. But this did not happen until much later in life. On February 14, 2011, I walked into my office preoccupied with the idea that Valentine's Day, or Black Love Day (which is how my husband and I have renamed the day) should be an official holiday—a day where people all over the world can freely express love and take the day off from work. As I walked to my office, one of my staff members stood in the hallway. He was waiting for me. I thought, "What now, another crisis or emergency?" I guess I was already pretty irritable, or perhaps emotionally drained.

Working in mental health can be depleting. As a therapist you are in the position of listening to the most horrific stories often back to back, with very little reprieve. Yet I could have never imagined what my colleague was about to tell me.

"Maysa, I have some sad news, Jocelyn (our receptionist and one of my most adored employees) was stabbed multiple times by her estranged husband."

I was in pure shock. I could not speak. The stack of books and papers I held in my hands dropped to the floor. The only thing that kept me standing was the wall. With my body numb, my heart racing, and my thoughts spinning in a million directions, I began sweating, became lightheaded, and within a few moments began to sob. I wept with the deepest pain you could ever imagine. My belly ached, I felt nauseous, and my heart pounded out of my chest. I felt complete despair rush through my body, as I wept uncontrollably and inconsolably.

Jocelyn was special to me. She understood me and worked very hard to make my life as comfortable as possible so I could be an effective leader. She studied me, learned my habits, anticipated my needs, and loved me with all her heart. I felt the same emotional connection to her. She was special, but I also knew she was very troubled. She was like me, and many others, in the midst of her own Urban Trauma—growing up poor, on welfare, and with little opportunity. She had two young boys and was in a very abusive relationship. She had finally decided that she wanted better for herself and that she was going to leave her abusive husband, file a restraining order, and try to start her life anew. I fully supported her decisions. I encouraged her to move on, I shared my story and demonstrated that with determination, she too could be successful, she could make it, just the way I did.

But I was wrong.

I was so wrong. Jocelyn did not make it. According to the news coverage, she was stabbed eighteen times by her husband and strangled to death. She died on the scene, at the house she shared with her husband prior to moving out. Jocelyn told a co-worker earlier that evening that she was going to stop by her house to pick up her mail after leaving work. Apparently, her husband was waiting for her and intended to kill her on Valentine's Day.

This incident was my breaking point. It was the moment when I could not endure or witness one more traumatic event in my life. It was the moment when I questioned my sanity and my ability to really get through yet another loss. I had lost so much throughout my life. I was completely broken, and did not have the resources to pull myself together. We had a grief counselor come in to talk and support the staff. She spent a great deal of time supporting me through my grief and other life-changing events that were happening during that time. In one particular session she asked me about my childhood. For the first time someone was asking me about my experiences, about my feelings, about my thoughts, and about my pain. My emotional floodgates opened, as this incident unlocked memories that I had buried so deep. I remember that moment so clearly, as the therapist said, "Maysa, you know you have PTSD."

Post-Traumatic Stress Disorder (PTSD) was added to the third edition of the *Diagnostic and Statistical Manual of Mental Disorders* (*DSM-III*) in the 1980s. The *DSM* is considered by many as the "bible" for mental health professionals. It is a resource that uses terms to categorize people who have similar symptoms into different diagnostic formulations. Symptoms for various disorders may overlap, but a mental health professional has to use their best clinical judgment to see which one is the best fit. There are times when the categorization is not one-dimensional, so clients may have multiple diagnoses.

From a historical perspective, the original definition of PTSD required that the origin was outside the individual (i.e., a traumatic event) rather than within the person (i.e., chemical imbalances). As you would expect, the key to understanding PTSD is the concept of "trauma."

In its initial *DSM-III* formulation, a traumatic event was conceptualized as a catastrophic stressor that was outside the range of usual human experience. The National Center for PTSD, the framers of the original PTSD diagnosis, had in mind events such as war, torture, rape, the Holocaust, the atomic bombings of Hiroshima and Nagasaki, natural disasters (such as earthquakes, hurricanes, and volcano eruptions), and human-made disasters (such as factory explosions, airplane crashes, and automobile accidents). *Take note:* slavery is never mentioned when you look for historical definitions of trauma.

People thought of traumatic events as different from the very painful everyday stressors that could be considered normal changes in life, such as marital conflict, multiple life failures, abandonment/rejection, medical conditions, and financial problems. Back then, these stressful events were not considered traumatic at all. The difference between trauma and other stressors was based on the theory that most individuals have the ability to cope with ordinary stress. However, people's adaptive capacities, emotional stability, and social functioning are likely to be overwhelmed when confronted by a serious traumatic stressor. As the research community better understood the etiology of PTSD, its definition has changed. This is most evident in the recent revision of the *Diagnostic and Statistical Manual of Mental Disorders—* called *DSM-5* and published in 2013—where significant changes were made to the diagnosis of PTSD. The most notable change is that it is no longer classified as an Anxiety Disorder, and is instead now categorized as a Trauma and Stressor Related Disorder. This change was implemented to remove the focus of PTSD away from anxiety symptoms and to look at trauma specifically, in the absence of anxiety.

Today, trauma is more broadly defined, not just as a fear-based disorder, but instead as a condition consisting of an anhedonic/dysphoric presentation, with negative cognitions and mood states, as well as disruptive (e.g., angry, impulsive, reckless, and self-destructive) behavioral symptoms. These symptoms are also identified as a response to a catastrophic event involving actual or threatened death or injury; a threat to the physical integrity (such as sexual violence) of that person or to others; or witnessing an event (e.g., innocent bystander). This also includes repeated, indirect exposure—usually as part of one's professional responsibilities—to the gruesome and horrific consequences of a traumatic event (often experienced by police personnel, body handlers, and EMTs).

Although I have laid out the definition of PTSD, it is important to understand that while you can experience a traumatic event, it does not necessarily mean that you will become symptomatic or meet the criteria for PTSD—every individual is different. Based on my story above would you say I experienced a traumatic event? You are right, I definitely experienced multiple traumatic events, in fact many before and after that one. But I did not become symptomatic at that time. I did not become symptomatic until Jocelyn's death.

For this reason, I want to make the key distinction between PTSD and Urban Trauma. Through my personal life experiences and having the privilege of becoming intimately involved with the lives of many others who have shared their stories with me, I personally believe that many of us who are from communities of color experience Urban Trauma, but do not become symptomatic or develop PTSD—at least not right away. That does not mean that we don't sometimes use negative methods, such as addiction and substance abuse, to cope with our situations. It just means that we do not have a defined clinical disorder.

A Timeline of Historical Traumatic Events Against Black People

Historically there have been many traumatic events that have shaped civilizations and social structures leading to Urban Trauma:

1501-1774	12.5 million Africans shipped to the New World; 388,000 to North America
1522	Slave Revolt: The Caribbean Slaves rebel in Hispaniola (Haiti/Dominican Republic)
1619	Twenty African slaves brought to Jamestown, Virginia
1775-1865	Abolitionist movement; thousands of slaves died fighting for freedom
1846-1928	Convict Leasing
1850	Fugitive Slave Act
1861-1865	American Civil War
1863	Emancipation Proclamation
1865-1868	Black Codes
1877-1954	Jim Crow
1882-1968	Lynching
1932-1972	Medical Experimentation
1937	Redlining
1950	Voter ID (special ID laws that limit voter rights)
1951	Mandatory Minimum Sentencing (established with the Boggs Act of 1951)
1951	*Brown v. Board of Education* (class action suit to end racial segregation in schools)
1954-1968	Civil Rights Movement

Racism Reinvented

1963	Gentrification
1966	1/3 of Black Americans live in poverty
1966	*Green v. Board of Elections* (U.S. Supreme Court found tax polls unconstitutional)
1967	Disenfranchisement
1968	*Terry v. Ohio* (beginning of Stop & Frisk; implemented fully in the1990s)
1969	Benign Neglect
1982-1986	Anti-Drug Abuse Act (War on Drugs-Reagan Administration)
1990	Zero Tolerance Policy (broken-window theory of policing)
1994	Three Strikes Law
1994	Gun-Free Schools Act (expulsion for infractions in or outside of school)
1994	Mass Incarceration
1996	HIV/AIDS Epidemic highest in Black Community
1997	School-to-Prison Pipeline (policing schools)
1998-2008	Privatizing Prisons
1999-Present Day	Institutional Racism Defined
2007-Present Day	Microaggression/Implicit Bias: New Face of Racism
2011-Present Day	Police Brutality Exposed
2017-	Public Education Under Attack

My prediction is that Urban Trauma will be perpetuated as education is targeted. I believe the current administration has already designed a way to dismantle public school education. (One can already start to see this with DeVos's policies and the monetary cuts in the public education sector.) Why would they do this, you ask? Education is the way out of poverty for many people of color. Unless you are discovered as an exceptional athlete, musician, or actor/actress, education (technical, post-secondary) is the ONLY ticket to the middle class. By dismantling the public education system there will be fewer and fewer opportunities for people like me to get through. Many will remain in poverty and without resources. Cycle on repeat.

From Slavery to the Pursuit of Freedom

Throughout history, Blacks in the Americas have endured continuous moments of devastating setbacks, limited progress and retaliation in the pursuit of freedom. Since the arrival of enslaved Africans in America in 1619, when twenty African slaves were captured and brought as cargo, Blacks have lived traumatic experiences throughout generations. It is important to address that while slavery existed all over the world prior to its inception in America, the expression of American slavery was by far the most brutal and savage form ever seen. By definition and through forms of behavior, slavery in Africa was closer to indentured servitude. When African tribe leaders sold off slaves to the Europeans they could never and would have never fathomed the severity in abuse and the dehumanization that would await slaves in the New World.

Slavery in America was created for one purpose and one purpose only: to build the American economic system and develop capitalism. The reality was brutal, bloody, and oppressing. Slavery was not meant for tribal domination like in Africa. It did not lead to eventual freedom. It was not just for labor. Instead slavery became a way for Europeans to show their control, power, and dominance over Black people all over the diaspora. For more than 300 plus years, men, women, and children were bought and sold for profit, thereby creating the economic foundation of America and the New World economy. Generations of Blacks remained in slavery and humans were considered property—and inventoried as such. According to the Trans-Atlantic Slave Trade Database, during the entire history of the slave trade to the New World (between 1525 and 1866), 12.5 million Africans were shipped to the New World. Only 10.7 million survived the dreaded Middle Passage, disembarking in North America, the Caribbean, and South America. And how many of these 10.7 million Africans were shipped directly to North America? Only about 388,000. That's right, a tiny percentage.

> **We need to acknowledge, accept, and validate that the institution of slavery created the first generation of a traumatized race of people who were victims of complex, chronic, and devastating traumatic experiences.**

According to Dr. Joy DeGruy author of *Post Traumatic Slave Syndrome,* "Of greatest import, the American slavery experience was exclusively based on the notion of racial inferiority. According to Thomas D. Morris in his book, *Southern Slavery and the Law 1619-1860,* Africans were considered to be 'presumed' or 'natural slaves' based on their skin color. They were also referred to as 'thinking property' and inherently 'rightless persons.' In few societies, if any, were so large a group of people considered to be less than human based on physical appearance. Yet Europeans concluded that enslaved Africans were fitted by a natural act of God to the position of permanent bondage. It was this relegation to lesser humanity that allowed the institution of chattel slavery, when slaves legally became property, to be intrinsically linked with violence, and it was through violence, aggression, and dehumanization that the institution of slavery was enacted, legislated, and perpetuated by Europeans." (DeGruy, 2005).

It is estimated that in the eighteenth century, six to seven million slaves were imported to North America. They accounted for more than one-third of the southern population and were completely dominated through fear, intimidation, and physical, emotional, and psychological abuse by their masters.

The existence of the Black slave by historical definition meant that every day was stressful and full of traumatic, often unspeakable, acts. For the slave, physical assault in the form of severe punishment, humiliation, sexual violence, and deprivation became a way of life. The slave system included various forms of restrictions and punishments designed to maintain control over Black people. Slaves were prohibited from engaging in any activity that would allow for mental advancement such as reading, writing, and voting. Masters took advantage of the slave women, raping them and having children with them. For this reason, chattel slavery in America is seen as a *cataclysmic traumatic experience*, the first of its kind and the most horrific in world history. Fully understanding these historical events gives us greater insight into the connection between the mental state of Black people today and the suffering of our ancestors dating back to 1619, when the first enslaved Africans were forcefully brought to Jamestown, Virginia. It is also important to recognize that the physical assault against our people was not enough to satisfy the European master. Instead, a more damaging psychological warfare was launched to ensure that generations of Blacks in America would question their rightful place in this world, challenge their self-concept, and even their very existence. As such, many more profound events emerged as a full-fledged racial war was launched against Black people. One that threatens our very existence.

Blacks in Bondage

From 1830 to 1860 a movement occurred to abolish slavery and free slaves. The Thirteenth Amendment was ratified late in 1865 "freeing" slaves. However, freedom was difficult—if not impossible—to obtain due to restrictive codes and regressive laws that kept newly freed slaves in bondage. A portion of that effort to keep Blacks enslaved and promote discrimination was Jim Crow laws and Black Codes. Jim Crow laws (1877-1954) were state and local laws that enforced racial segregation, particularly in Southern states. Jim Crow laws systematically mandated the segregation of public schools, public places, public transportation, as well as the segregation of restrooms, restaurants, and drinking fountains for Whites and Blacks. Black Code laws (1865-1868) in the United States were laws passed by Southern states in 1865 and 1866, after the Civil War. These laws had the intent and the effect of restricting the freedom of Black people, and of compelling them to work in a labor economy based on low wages or debt. Black Codes were part of a larger pattern of Southern Whites trying to suppress the new freedom of emancipated Black slaves. In large part, these laws were modeled after the pre-emancipation slave codes. The goal of the slave codes was to reduce influence of free Blacks (particularly after slave rebellions) because of their potential influence on slaves in bondage. Restrictions included prohibiting them from voting, bearing arms, gathering in groups for worship, and learning to read and write. A major purpose of these laws was to preserve slavery.

These degenerating laws produced social, economic, and political hardship for people of color. Furthermore, groups supporting institutionalized racism, such as the Ku Klux Klan and the Knights of the White Camellia, brought terror, violence, and voter suppression to Black communities. Reconstruction was ultimately frustrating for Black people due to these hardships. The resistance to lingering racism and discrimination in America that began in slavery would centuries later lead to a movement for equality. In 1954, the Supreme Court's *Brown v. Board of Education* decision struck down so-called separate-but-equal education and mandated that American schools be racially integrated. The Supreme Court unanimously ruled that separate educational facilities were inherently unequal and identified this arrangement as unconstitutional. In 1957, at the start of integration, nine students at Little Rock High School were harassed and spat upon. The humiliation for basic human rights was unfathomable. Following the desegregation in the school system, the National Association for the Advancement of Colored People (NAACP) hoped that desegregation would mean equal education for Black students, yet Blacks soon realized that the fight for equality would be continuous, and seemed never ending.

Colorism

Divide and conquer was the strategy used to separate critical masses from forming—vis-à-vis alliances between enslaved Africans, Natives, and poor Whites—to overturning slavery. Group dissension was also created among slaves by assigning distinctions between the field slave and the house slave. The house slave was typically lighter in complexion or the offspring of the slave master. As a result of racial mixing, colorism spawned. Since the inception of slavery, the idea that Black people are inferior to White people has been planted in our minds. That idea has morphed into a hierarchy among Black people, with those who more closely resemble White people at the top. In 1712, Willie Lynch, who was a British slave owner in the West Indies, allegedly wrote a letter to fellow slave owners. While some historians debate the authenticity of the Willie Lynch letter, many of the points outlined in the letter support the actions taken by Whites to perpetuate lasting effects of separatism, mental enslavement, and psychological control over Black people (to view the letter visit www.MaysaAkbar.com/WillieLynchLetter).

Although many Blacks experienced discrimination—overtly during slavery and through Jim Crow, and subtly until this very day—the intensity, the frequency, and generational impact of that discrimination differed dramatically based on skin tone. Colorism in the United States is rooted in slavery; it produced a strict distinction among the slaves that enforced division, disorganization, and disunity. White people managed to create dissension in such a deep-rooted way that enslavement became mental, permeating the mindset of our people for centuries. It continues to plague our communities to this day. Colorism is a powerful tool used to keep us divided. Interestingly, it wasn't until 1982 when Alice Walker coined the term "colorism" that she gave life to a phenomenon that was occurring among Black folks for centuries.

I have had a particularly hard time with colorism because I happen to be one of those light-skinned people who can easily "pass" as a member of many other cultures. It took me years to understand what my dark-skinned friends and family would tell me about the privilege that came along with my complexion. I would often reject this notion and become enraged by the mere suggestion that I was not as Black as any dark-skinned person. In addition, my self-image was incongruent with my outer appearance. In that, if being darker-skinned was directly tied to activism, advocacy, Black Power, and pride, then I should have been as dark as they came. Over the course of years and self-reflection, by truly listening to what folks had to say about this topic, I began to understand that my fight against their statements was causing more of a divide than a movement. It was important that I validated the experience of my dark-skinned brothers and sisters instead of dismissing the conversation. In reality, the dismissal came from my own insecurities about my complexion and perhaps my wish that my outer appearance reconciled with who I am and what I stand for on the inside. Once I dealt with those insecurities and did my research, I was able to have a more authentic conversation about color and race. To further illustrate the point, research demonstrates that fair-skinned people have more opportunity for better income, education, housing, and employment. Once we can have this type of open dialogue, it creates a space for collaboration and how we can all work together to battle the real threats in our community.

Recently, I engaged in a conversation about this very same topic with a dear friend and colleague Reverend Dr. Boise Kimber, an American Baptist minister and civil rights activist. I listened, validated, and understood his pain as a dark-skinned Black man growing up in the South, post-slavery, and during the segregation era. Dr. Kimber thinks that racism in the United States will never change. Dr. Kimber goes on to say, "This country was built upon racism. Things are getting better and we're talking about the issues, but when you still have the faith community not able to sit down and have conversations about race, you are going to have a hard time moving past and resolving major issues."

"Within the Black community there are different shades of Black. There was always high yella girls, and the high yella girls got seats; Black people like me, who looked more like slaves, were thought of as 'Mandingo warrior' types. This created—and still creates—tension within the community. The tension comes from the fact that one White man, somewhere down the line, slept with your great grandmother or grandmother to make you the color that you are. This produced a split because those who are high colored felt that if they adapted to the White man's premises, they would be accepted more than dark people. It's still the same now."

Centuries of Trauma

The reality of the Black experience in America is that as a people we have experienced trauma centuries before it was even called trauma. Past pain and present trauma is connected throughout the history of Blacks in America. How is Rodney King, a taxi driver who suffered facial fractures, a broken right ankle, and multiple bruises and lacerations after being violently beaten by police in 1991, different from Emmett Till, whose body was discovered—beaten and bloated—after he had "supposedly whistled" at a White woman in 1955? The 2015 racist hate crime and shooting of nine congregation members at Emmanuel African Methodist Episcopal (A.M.E) Church, in Charleston, North Carolina, clearly resembles the 1963 church bombing in Birmingham, Alabama, where four beautiful girls were killed because of hatred and white supremacy ideology.

Current issues around White privilege, the Black Lives Matter movement, awareness of microaggressions, and implicit bias are consequences of the unfinished equal rights agenda. All of these recent moments in history connect and interweave to tell a story of Black pain, disenfranchised communities, and systemic racism. Multigenerational trauma is a result of centuries of oppression, inequality, and injustice since the days of slavery. As a cultural process, Urban Trauma has the ability to form a collective identity for Black people (Eyerman, 2004). Racial trauma unites generations of people of color together by memory of past trauma, present representation, and the collective group identity.

Reverend Dr. Kimber goes on to say, the "legacy of slavery will always be with us. It's like the Holocaust with the Jews. They won't ever forget it. And even though there are people in our [Black] community who don't want to have the conversation about slavery, it's because they didn't hear enough about it, their parents didn't go through it. But I went through it. I understand it. Black folks ain't going to ever be free until they free their brothers and sisters along with them."

"Slavery has always been about mental bondage. We just started to really acknowledge in the twentieth century that we need help in dealing with our past. We need help with child abuse, sexual abuse, domestic violence, and people still dealing with past pain and how they were treated and what took place. We are dealing with that now. We are getting some assistance now," exclaimed Dr. Kimber.

The Broken Family

We learn about relationships through the first people we are exposed to: our family. If family is not within reach, we are left to our own imagination to create what we think relationships should look and feel like. The significance of family is one of the most essential necessities to humankind. Family is the educational platform where children obtain the necessary skills to socialize with others. Parents, for the most part, are necessary agents in teaching their child many first moments—most importantly, how to interact with the world. Children learn how to talk, walk, and behave from their parents. Independence, morals, mannerisms, and a host of other characteristics originate from families. Values that children are taught come directly from the environment the parents live in, which can facilitate or hinder a child's integration (or survival) in that environment or others. Family is where rules and norms for essential coexistence are developed. Those rules and norms form the way children will operate with others. They also dictate their successful integration and interaction with society. For these reasons, family is also the place where we learn basic things, such as respect, manners, appearance, and conduct. The old adage "the apple does not fall far from the tree" describes the function of family perfectly. Tell me who you are, and I will tell you about your family.

Given the tribal nature of our African ancestors it is in our DNA to be connected to the world by virtue of relationships. We are a "feeling" people that typically operate from a place of interconnectedness. Beyond our experience in this country, we can trace back to our African roots and heritage, the traditions of tribal communities and a familial way of life. When the relationships in the tribe are disrupted, we are not right with ourselves, others, or the world. Many may feel conflicted, edgy, frustrated, and confused, but mostly angry. If we are instinctually tribal by nature, what happens to relationships that have turned abusive and when that abuse is reinforced by the society we live in?

In order for us change generational cycles of trauma, we have to understand the role family plays in keeping trauma alive and well.

Throughout history, the Black family has been consistently faced with challenges that brought forth division, strife, and disunity among family members and the community. Even in this century, it is not unusual for Black children to be born to an unwed mother and grow up in a single parent home. In 2008, President Obama reported that only 40% of Black children live with their father in the home. The other 60% live in a single parent household, many in poverty and struggling to survive. Disenfranchised Black families are typically categorized with having high rates of drug addiction, welfare dependency, teenage pregnancy, and single woman households (Sampson, 1987). Basic developmental psychology tells us that boys and girls growing up without fathers and in unstable homes are overwhelmingly more likely to lack self-discipline and personal responsibility, than children growing up with married parents or two parents. Consequences of the disrupted Black family can include poverty, educational deficiencies, violence, and crime. Historically, the division in the Black family structure was foreshadowed during slavery.

Slavery and Family Instability

Many researchers claim that the current disorganization and instability in the Black family was a result of common practices during slavery (DuBois, 1899, 1909; Elkins, 1963; Frazier, 1932, 1939; Myrdal, 1944). Black people were not seen as individuals with rights and purpose but as property with taxes attached to them. They weren't even able to own their name, let alone have a voice or maintain family ties. During the period of American slavery, Blacks were denied privileges such as the right to join together as husband and wife, in the traditional sense. To make up for this lack, many began to create and construct their own traditions. The formal joining of the slave couple was then solemnized by symbolically jumping over a household broomstick, giving us the present-day term of "jumping the broom" (Goring, 2005).

The constant disruption and division of the Black family during slavery was and remains undeniably traumatizing. Children were separated from parents, wives from husbands, and siblings from each other without a second thought. For instance, Black men could not be a father figure for their children or take on the role of husband for their wife (Wilson, 2002). Children were easily taken away from their parents and sold to slaveholders as workers, usually on a plantation farther away from their original place of birth. Due to the frequent replacing and removing of family members, the Black community had to create their own family system to fuel the community. They responded by creating kinships to create a sense of family when unable to consistently be surrounded by biological family. "Kin" refers to any relative by blood, marriage, or close non-family ties that form a family unit (Scannapieco & Jackson, 1996). Through kinship, the community collectively took care of one another and raised children in the tradition of the old African proverb "It takes a village to raise a child." Women were automatically given responsibility for nurturing and supporting children who were new to the plantation. Additionally, women faced many hardships on the plantation during slavery. Many were sexually assaulted and raped in order to procreate. Sometimes slaveholders would force the men and women to have sex in order to birth children to sell. This was done for money and greed since, by consistently selling children, slaveholders increased their property value. And since Black women were the property of their masters, they could be used any way that they pleased (Tolman, 2011). This disruption in the slave community made it difficult for a cohesive family unit to exist.

Once slaves were given freedom, there was still a struggle for the existence of the Black family. After they were freed, thousands of former slaves set out to reunite with their relatives whose families had been dissolved by sale and distance. Some slaves had been sold so often or so long before emancipation that family members no longer had reliable information as to their relatives' whereabouts. There were endless roadblocks in the path of former slaves that did not allow for the Black family to unite.

This wound of the forcibly broken family, however, continues to the present day. Fathers who were unable to be fathers, had children who couldn't be fathers. Women lost trust in their men because as many men battled the demons of their past, they became emotionally disconnected and some became abusive. The sanctity of the Black family was hard to preserve when there was no example of how to do so. Despite the very best intentions, it became and at times continues to be very difficult to cultivate strong Black family units, particularly in poor communities.

With all these odds stacked against us, it is no wonder that it is so hard for some Black families to stay intact. Black folks are not just fighting the typical challenges to keep their marriage together, they are also fighting against the disruption of the Black family that became commonplace tradition for hundreds of years since slavery. Every day we work to reconstruct and rebuild what was torn to pieces in our families. For many, Urban Trauma results in Black men feeling displaced, Black women feeling abandoned, and children who are confused by the lack of a stable family unit.

Father Hunger

I firmly believe that if you want to support the growth and development of the male child, find a way for him to be on good terms with his father and keep him engaged. To be clear, marriage is not required in order for a father to remain actively involved in a child's life. The mere fact that there are gender differences suggests that there are fundamental aspects of male socialization that mothers will not be able to do well—from the most basic, such as how to use a toilet, to the more complex, such as sexual development.

In the absence of a good male role model, our young men will feed off of images on television, listen to the lyrics of their favorite rapper, and—right or wrong—adapt these characteristics as their own. If you are open to exploring this, ask a young boy, a teen, or an adult man who lacks a father if he misses his father? Ask him what he misses the most? If he had one wish related to his father, what would that be? What would he tell his dad? What does he hunger for the most?

Father hunger has been defined as receiving too little quality fathering as a child or young adult. Some argue that even grown men and women need fathers, or father surrogates, and that the absence of such role modeling and support is associated with less fulfillment in life and can contribute to Urban Trauma. In general, father hunger results from too little intimacy between a child and its father.

My colleague Dr. Brett Rayford, who works with adolescent boys, introduced me to the term "father hunger." His feeling is that for Black boys, the absence of a father has lasting effects that not only impacts them, but also the choices they will make when it comes to fathering and raising their own children.

I recall a Black male patient telling me that he has been angry his whole life, for as long as he could remember. When I asked him to try to recall the first time he remembers feeling angry, he was able to tell me with a great level of specificity that it was the day he waited—dressed, excited, and ready to go—for his father, who never showed up. This happened time after time. Eventually, he said, "I stopped crying," and he began to teach himself how to become cold and disconnected, to never be vulnerable and to put up a "brick wall" so no one would hurt him again. He said this with pride, as if he had come up with a great solution for his problem. He spoke about moments when he connects with his anger and how they have been best buddies ever since childhood. I asked him how that was working out for him, he chuckled as he said, "Well I am here seeing a therapist, aren't I?" This is a story retold by many Black men who feel the emotional pain associated with father hunger, and are now so emotionally unavailable that they are unable to have loving relationships. This is because in healthy relationships vulnerability must exist—with their spouses, partners, parents, family, and children.

We must remember that those living with Urban Trauma have the power to change any and all circumstances. I have known many brave Black men who have broken the cycle of father hunger, of violence, of abuse, of abandonment, despite lacking a father. Many make the effort to be a better father to their children. It starts with finding the right support to do this with another male role model.

PART I

Section Two: Poverty, Community Violence, and Educational Disparities

POVERTY

The Fight for Freedom

The end of slavery was thought to have been the beginning of freedom for many Blacks in America. However, many Blacks were soon to discover that although their status had transitioned from being slaves to being free, White society still treated them as "less than." In an effort to subordinate Blacks and enforce White supremacy, Jim Crow laws were constructed in the south (Kousser, 2003). This new era enforced social, economic, and political discrimination to keep segregation thriving in the midst of the fight for freedom (Kousser, 2003). White Americans were treated in a superior manner in the community, school system, restaurants, and in matters of real estate. Blacks were treated so unfairly, they were denied the right to ride in the front of public transportation, eat at certain restaurants, and attend schools with White students (Edwards & Thomson, 2010). By 1915, Jim Crow laws and Southern hostility became the norm. It wasn't long before those radical enough to truly fight for their freedom knew that it was time for a call to action. In response to the increase in prejudice, discrimination, and violence, Black leaders created the National

Association for the Advancement of Colored People (NAACP) in 1909. The NAACP led the long effort to overturn Jim Crow laws and all that threatened the Black community.

However, even with the support of this organization, it was still a struggle to enforce the Black community's right to vote. Keeping Blacks out of the polling booth was essential for maintaining White dominance. When acts of prejudice and segregation did not work, brutal acts of violence, terror, and educational stipulations were used to scare off the Black voter. For example, barring former prisoners, barring those who were illiterate, the implementation of poll taxes, and the purging of the voting poll decreased the number of Black voters. These voting barriers, along with gerrymandering (manipulation of the polling districts to establish a political advantage), made it that much more difficult for Blacks to have a say within their districts. As a result of these efforts, in Louisiana the voter registration of Blacks went from 130,000 in 1896 to 1,300 in 1905 (Packard, 2002).

Despite the struggle for equality, there were moments of progress and proactivity within the Black community toward establishing political gain. In 1921, Tulsa, Oklahoma, became one of the most wealthy and progressive communities for Blacks in the United States. Black residents were not only wealthy, but they were Black businessmen, lawyers, and doctors who wanted to give back to their community. They became known as the "Black Wall Street." What started as progress, however, did not last long. One resident of the Tulsa community was accused of raping a young White woman, which led to an outbreak of racial violence. White rioters began looting, burning buildings, and assaulting Black people who lived in that district. The result was a massacre led by the Ku Klux Klan. It's been estimated that more than 40 square blocks of Black-owned homes, hospitals, school, churches, and businesses were destroyed. This is an example of Black people—against all odds—trying to create the American Dream as a community, but at every turn, those attempts were met with fierce opposition, violence, and destruction.

As if external racial violence was not enough, within the Black community there were—and still are—moments of regression, discrimination, and stereotyping. Colorism resulted in many lighter-skinned Blacks feeling entitled to a different type of treatment from society. This sense of entitlement extended beyond slavery and into the Black community. The lighter the complexion, the more privilege and access to social advantages (Banks, 1999). The socioeconomic, employment, and achievement gap between light- and dark-skinned Blacks became equivalent to the gap that existed between Whites and all Blacks in general (Seltzer & Smith, 1991; Udry, Bauman, & Chase, 1971). Furthermore, as the Black community began to gain access to privileges that were withheld from them while they were enslaved, the privilege gap between light and dark-skinned Blacks continued to widen. So much so that in the South, there were churches, community organizations and Black Greek organizations that denied entry to Black people whose skin color was darker than a brown paper bag (Hall, 1992). What started off as a color-code hierarchy in slavery has evolved into intra-racial discrimination and prejudice. Anything that threatens the collective group identity of the Black community creates division. Another form of division is created through "borderism"—discrimination against those individuals who are considered to be "sellouts" for "acting white." (Busey, 2014). Choosing to be different and standing apart from typical Black behavior and the collective racial identity labeled you as an outcast. Whether it was internal or external oppression, Blacks have faced an insurmountable level of adversity since they were forced to set foot on U.S. soil.

To further illustrate this point let's discus how poverty, violence, and educational disparities have been used to further support White supremacy. There is a perfect analogy that I like to use when I do diversity trainings and the topic of equality vs. equity. It was a story that I heard once from a speaker addressing health equity in communities of color. She mentioned in her talk that she likes to garden. She made a connection between the struggle of Black people in America and gardening because I suppose that she wanted to make her message palatable. The story goes like this: Let's say you have two flower boxes, one you have prepared for pink roses and the other for red roses. The roses are different, unique in their own way, but there is nothing that makes one superior over the other. The only major difference is color. The red roses, however, are planted in the rich, fertilized soil you get from a gardening store. The pink roses are planted in leftover soil from the backyard. Both roses are planted with care, both have adequate sunshine, both are watered daily, and nurtured. When it is time for them to bloom, there is a distinct difference between them. The red roses are well-rooted, blooming nicely, growing strong, tall, and standing proud among the other roses in the box. The pink roses have a different look. There are some pink ones that were able to grow tall and strong, but the majority of them were small, frail, with only a few petals, and the amount of roses in that box was sparse. What is the difference in the example? You guessed it, the soil. If you consider the "soil" that Black people have stepped into since being forced into this country doesn't it make sense that our urban communities look like the pink rose box? Some of us make it, the majority struggle fighting to survive (in a country whose soil is filled with hate, racism, oppression, bigotry, violence, prejudice, and discrimination). So even if all things were really equal for Black people, which we know they are not, true equity begins with the root of the problem, the soil (i.e., institutionalized racism). Therefore, the nutrient deficient soil is a symbol for lack of equity rooted in racism. Until we till (dig, stir, and overturn) the soil we will never see equity for our people.

Perpetual Disadvantage Across Generations

Since equity seemed unattainable, we dedicated our fight for equality and progression. However, racial and ethnic discrimination continued to exist for Blacks throughout the twentieth century. From the 1940s to the 1960s, inner city neighborhoods were integrated with lower-, working-, and middle-class Black families. They were forced into overcrowded, neglected neighborhoods through violence, prejudice, and discriminatory practices by real estate agents (Dunlap, Golub, & Johnson, 2006). Upon receiving an application, real estate agents and rental property managers discriminated against people of color, which further established neighborhood inequality, a practice called redlining. It was common for racial background to determine where one lived, as well as the privileges they would be capable of receiving. Housing took on a pattern that utilized segregation to form concentrated poverty (Squires & Kubrin, 2005). Socioeconomic status of applicants held no weight. If you were Black or Latino you were placed in a disadvantaged community and completely isolated. These high-poverty neighborhoods were filled with members of minority groups, creating the continuation of racial and ethnic segregation. The majority of residents had to deal with poverty, violence, and injustice (Kuo, 2001). Basic things like grass and a play area for the kids were removed, and in places like New York City, public housing was referred to as the "concrete jungle" for that reason.

Consequences brought from this selective gentrification were deprivation, incarceration, injury, and even death (Kuo, 2001). Despite the Fair Housing Act of 1968 prohibiting discrimination concerning the sale, rental, and financing of housing based on race, religion, national origin, and sex, residential segregation persisted through the 1970s and 1980s. Lending practices imposed unfair lending terms on people of color. Many of the borrowers were unable to afford what was being asked of them, which led to payment plans with higher interest rates and a large amount of debt. Racial and class seclusion slowly created inner city projects that brought forth a collective identity for many Black people. The poorer the neighborhood, the more prevalent unemployment became, lowering the socioeconomic class of its residents. Residing in these high-poverty neighborhoods exacerbated problems such as education, employment, and development of skills needed to succeed. As a result, housing policy has been criticized for contributing to the concentration of poverty, race, and social problems in urban communities (Jargowsky, 2014). The Section 8 program was one policy response to the growing problem of poverty concentration in public housing.

> Concentrated poverty, racism, and residential segregation are the key factors in the plight of the Black urban poor.

To boot, once the community was held hostage by drugs, the barriers that prevented Black families from making it out of the 'hood grew. Not only did Blacks struggle with affordable housing while living in impoverished areas within the inner city, they also faced additional hardship with the introduction of drugs. For example, between the 1980s and 1990s crack cocaine was distributed throughout major cities and towns in the United States such as New York, Los Angeles, and Chicago. Low-income, urban, minority neighborhoods suffered not only from the drugs, but from the violence and crime rate that came with it (Fryer, et al., 2005). Urban Blacks became the most burdened by concentrated socioeconomic disadvantage. Also known as the "Crack Era", the introduction of cocaine led to a spike in violence, prostitution, abuse, and corruption (Dunlap, Golub, & Johnson, 2006). Within the Black family, crack represented a major distraction contributing to child abuse, neglect, and abandonment of parental responsibilities.

Economically, the 1970s was a particularly difficult period for inner city families. Many residents were unqualified for emerging opportunities because of their lack of education, low income, and lack of employment. The drug market was easily accessible and more rewarding. While it was difficult for individuals in the community to gain employment, the high price of drugs brought in multiple streams of income. Thus, selling drugs became a way of economic survival. Drug sales established criminal networks throughout the country, and those networks capitalized on the enormous profits earned from the trafficking and selling of crack cocaine, heroin, and other drugs. While the War on Drugs started during the Nixon administration, Michelle Alexander did a masterful job of explaining in her 2012 book *The New Jim Crow* that in 1982, President Ronald Reagan declared the drug war against crack before crack had actually become an issue. She theorizes that Reagan's war on drugs was declared far before drugs truly became an epidemic, suggesting that there was some level of intentionality around purposefully implanting drugs in Black urban communities. Alexander surmises that the War on Drugs and all of the associated consequences including mass incarceration could in fact be the new Jim Crow. In 2016, journalist Dan Baum exposed what could be considered confirmation of Alexander's hypothesis when he quoted John Ehrlichman's (White House Domestic Affairs Advisor, 1969-1973) earnest response about drugs and politics during the

Nixon administration: "We knew we couldn't make it illegal to be either against the war or Black [people], but by getting the public to associate the hippies with marijuana and Blacks with heroin, and then criminalizing both heavily, we could disrupt those communities. We could arrest their leaders, raid their homes, break up their meetings, and vilify them night after night on the evening news. Did we know we were lying about the drugs? Of course we did."

By 1980, the increase in crack sales and the establishment of the drug market brought about an attendant wave of violence. This spread of crack sales can be traced back to the gang members' family ties in these cities, and to the lure of quick profits (more on this in the community violence section). Although the real money makers were the distributors, money derived from narcotic sales soon became the symbol of power and status. Being a part of the gang family offered advantages such as protection, a controlled territory in which to sell, resources, and entrance into the drug market (Decker & Van Winkle, 1994).

The consequence of placing Black people into inner city ghettos and introducing them to drugs led to the spread of disease. When HIV and AIDS first appeared in the Black community in the 1980s it was mostly due to intravenous drug use, prostitution, and other criminal activity (Dunlap, Golub, & Johnson, 2006). What seemingly started off as an epidemic among gay White men quickly became a plague in the Black community of all sexes and sexual orientations by 1996 (Hendricks & Wilson, 2013). The disproportionate impact of HIV and AIDS on Black Americans has its roots in poverty and severe disadvantages in the urban communities, where the epidemic has had its most enduring impact. Issues include increased demands on social services, the health care system, and the criminal justice system, as well as the loss of human life. Access to, use of, and quality of health care varies by socioeconomic status. Health inequity continues to threaten Black citizens in that they do not have fair and equal access to health care, medication, and preventative medicine. There is a high level of over-utilization of emergency rooms to treat common medical conditions that are now easily addressed in outpatient medical practices.

Residential segregation and neighborhood quality were the perfect ingredients to support racial disparities in health. (Williams & Chiquita, 2001). Those residing in low-income communities lacked resources as well as the proper health and dental care to manage their medical needs. In order for the government to eliminate health disparities, attention would have to be paid to the different factors that affect socioeconomic status. In addition to the disparity in healthcare was disparity in access to food. Research suggests that neighborhood residents who have better access to supermarkets and limited access to convenience stores tend to have healthier diets and lower levels of obesity. Further research illustrates that certain supermarkets, fast food restaurants, and liquor stores tend to be concentrated in neighborhoods according to their racial and socioeconomic pattern (Larson, Story, & Nelson, 2009).

Throughout history we see the connection between overcrowded housing, poor physical and mental health, despair, urban trauma, violence, crime, and drug abuse that exists in the inner city. These conditions made it difficult for Black families to succeed. Ask yourself, how could anyone survive these circumstances, let alone thrive? In the case of Black Americans, not only has the metaphorical soil been sparse, but all the other supplies needed to rebuild have been limited to non-existent at best. Particularly since growth has been met with significant challenge and opposition. Unfortunately, not much has changed; many poor Black young adults today have taken on the structural disadvantages of their parents and are unprepared to create and sustain change in their generation. Families exist today that are still battling the factors and barriers set before them, perpetuating disadvantage across generations.

A Face of Urban Trauma: Jamal

People who live in poverty appear to be at higher risk for mental illnesses. Poverty disproportionately affects the Black community, due in part to the legacy of slavery, segregation, and racial discrimination in America. Poverty also affects mental health. In 1966, four in ten (41.8%) of Black Americans were poor. Blacks constituted nearly a third (31.1%) of all poor Americans. By 2012, poverty among Blacks had fallen to 27.2%—still more than double the rate among Whites (12.7%). Furthermore, people experiencing homelessness are at an even greater risk of developing a mental health condition and most definitely are exposed to Urban Trauma (more on this in the second section of the book). Blacks make up 40% of the homeless population. The resulting challenges of poverty including hunger, difficulty finding jobs, homelessness, and lack of other vital needs, can be destabilizing. These living conditions can create a vicious cycle. Poverty increases the risk for mental health issues, which may then render an individual unable to work and afford basic needs, including treatment (Desilver, 2014).

Jamal's story is one that is heard all too often. People who live in poverty and those who become homeless are often not there by choice. Some folks do and want all the "right" things: they want a job, they want to advance in life, and want to do better for themselves. But as we have seen throughout this book, opportunities were and are more difficult to achieve for many Black people.

Jamal joined the military and served his country for two and a half years. When he was medically discharged and returned home, he found it difficult to fit back into society. A man who always worked hard, with technical engineering and mechanical skills and experience in repairing cars and other vehicles, he was confident he would find work. Employers were anxious to meet him when they received his resume, but when he went for the interview, he was told the job was filled, the specs had changed, or that he was over qualified. Jamal felt that his appearance as a Black man, and the stigma around veterans having PTSD were working against him. He worked where he could, doing oil changes and small repair jobs. He maximized the benefits of the VA for healthcare and medical services, used the food pantry, and other resources. But pride kept him from being "one of those veterans who just uses the system."

Jamal explained, "I didn't want to be on the corner begging. I didn't want to feel like an outcast. Or that I was trying to use somebody. I wanted to do it on my own. I didn't want anyone else's help. I didn't ask for a handout. I tried my best to hide [my homelessness] from everyone that was close to me. I was full of shame. My family didn't know anything about it until I came out of it. My friends didn't know anything. One day one of my friends asked me what was wrong with my fingernails and I shared with her my situation."

Jamal lived in his car and stayed with people from church and did some couch surfing with friends for short stays. The military provided him with a pre-paid membership to a local gym, where Jamal took showers, did his laundry, and stayed physically strong. He did small jobs and ate at fast food restaurants, because when you are homeless nutritious meals are just not possible.

"I felt like I had hit rock bottom. I didn't see a light. I didn't see how I would get out of it. But I was determined to scratch myself out. I was scared. I felt hopeless. I was very depressed. But I never thought I had the opportunity to give up. I couldn't give up. Something inside kept me going. I needed to survive." **This is Urban Trauma.**

Jamal admits that he didn't plan well when exiting the military. He didn't think about what he would do when he got out. He assumed that with a background in auto mechanics, engineering, and military service, he would be fine. "As a veteran with medical discharge, people look at you as broken. Usually they're worried about PTSD. They automatically cast you out because they fear you can't control your anger or rage. You get that stereotype as a Black man as well. So I had two counts against me, even though I had just put my life on the line for my country and to protect the freedom of all Americans."

Jamal said, "There are definitely people that are in worse situation than I was. There are those that can't get out of the hole they are in. I was better off because at least I had access to the VA. I knew where to go for help. A lot of people don't have health care, don't have medical, don't have the VA, so their situations are a lot worse than mine were."

Now that Jamal is back on his feet he is working with young Black adolescents in a mentor program called VETTS™. VETTS™ was designed to match honorably discharged military veterans with high-risk, at times gang-involved inner city youth. Jamal recalled one teenager he works with who is currently homeless. Jamal describes Joey as one of his most difficult mentoring cases. "This young man feels like he's a caretaker. He's close with his sister. He feels he needs to protect her. He would lay his life down on the line to protect her. He helped her to get a place. He is still in high school so he really couldn't get a job to help pay the rent. Social Security helped pay the bills but his sister couldn't do much. She wasn't able to work. She had a child she had to care for. They got evicted from three places within a year. Joey was sleeping in hallways, alleys, and still got ready for school the next morning.

At one point, Joey got a ticket for squatting in an apartment after eviction. He didn't give back the key when he got evicted, so he would go into the home he was evicted from and stay there. His sister and niece were able to stay in a homeless shelter but because he was over the age of fourteen, he wasn't allowed to go with them. The police came and arrested him for trespassing. The system is so punitive. Instead of understanding his poverty situation, homelessness, trying to make it and graduate from high school, they're punishing him. That arrest led to a warrant. At court Joey told the judge what he did and why, and he thankfully got a good judge who dismissed all charges. I was worried that Joey would go to jail just because he needed a place to sleep. That's the fate of Black men in our society today." **This is Urban Trauma.**

Jamal admitted "this situation triggered me a little. I stayed up all night. I cried. I felt what he was going through."

Joey has a lot of pride and wouldn't let Jamal help him, wouldn't tell Jamal where he was, because he felt the same way Jamal did after leaving the military: that he would get out of this himself, but also full of shame and traumatized by his current situation. Jamal has told Joey that he is not alone. He has help and can do this. He wanted to help Joey get into Job Corps, go the military route, get an education. Jamal is hopeful that Joey will have income and housing and stability soon.

Community Violence

Gangs—The Surrogate Family

As violence and criminal activity increased in the Black community, the formation of gangs began to shift. Gang formation was a result of the high volume of poverty concentrated in one area. Gangs were established from the need for safety, valued identity, and a sense of community (McMilan, Chavis, 1986). What started off as simply a provision of emotional support and physical security had transformed into functioning criminal enterprises with features of highly structured organizations (Alonso, 2004). Most people do not know that gangs were started to protect the Black community, not to terrorize it. Gangs typically hold respect, fraternity, trust, and loyalty to each other as well as to their neighborhood. At times, gangs established with a territorial identity, which extended the initiation into such groups across generations. It allowed, for those who needed it, an extended family and a way of ensuring income. By the early 1980s, gangs had sprung up in most of the large cities in the nation, especially concentrated in the poorer inner city and ring-city areas. Ring-city areas surround the city where the residents live mostly below the poverty line. Many saw a business opportunity within the drug industry and they took advantage of it. Remember: poverty and oppression are the mother and father of violence.

As gang formation heightened, so did the distribution of drugs and the nation's need for police intervention. Local police troops were encouraged to suppress gang crime and intercede whenever necessary. Many would try to solve the issue by increasing arrests and applying pressure on anyone who was suspected to be involved with gangs. It was at this moment that many gang members and individuals living in inner city communities began to distrust the police. Once that sense of protection was removed there was a division between police and gang members. More violence, strife, and disorganization entered into the urban community. By 1980, gangs and gang crime were identified as the cause of many of the nation's issues within the Black community and put on notice (Katz, Webb & Armstrong, 2003). This public fear of crime and gangs led to political campaigns focused on implementing harsher laws and punishment to invoke change (Lane & Meeker, 2003). The rising numbers of youths being killed and families being robbed shook the nation. In addition, the media's portrayal of gangs often depicted urban settings, blaming gangs for either harming the community or having gang-related activity (Lane, 1998). This brought about the legislation enforcing stop and frisk, zero tolerance policy, and the militarization of local police. In order to get a better handle on the utilization and selling of drugs, police implemented strategies such as house raiding and the increased use of SWAT teams (Cooper, 2015). Police intervention was established solely to arrest individuals after being notified that the individual had a high probable reason to be arrested. However, due to higher demand of action by politicians, police were able to stop someone based on probable cause. This led to an increase in police stopping and frisking Black and Latino men (Cooper, 2015). There was less talking, or de-escalation and an increase of physical force.

A Face of Urban Trauma: Kyisha

According to the National Center for PTSD, community violence is complex and can be inclusive of events that include but are not limited to "riots, attacks, gangs, drive-by shootings, assaults, terrorist attacks, torture, bombings, war, ethnic cleansing, and widespread sexual, physical, and emotional abuse." Community violence has recently been distinguished from other types of trauma. One such factor is that community violence usually happens without warning and comes as a sudden and terrifying shock. In light of this, fear and hypervigilance are heightened and safety is compromised, since violence can happen at any time. Another factor that makes community violence different is the widespread impact it has in permanently demolishing entire communities. The last differentiator is the intentionality behind community violence versus other types of trauma which can be accidental. The lasting effects for those who witness community violence are feelings of betrayal and distrust toward other people. I interviewed a colleague and friend who beat the odds of community violence and decided to get into the field of psychology in order to help those in the community.

Kyisha is an open-minded, educated, unique, and funny woman who grew up in an urban environment. Born and raised in New Haven, Connecticut, Kyisha explained, "When you grow up in an inner city, your world is much smaller than everybody else's world. The way you think of where you're from is by street, by neighborhood. The confusion comes in that when you're young you only identify with a specific population. Not even with all Blacks. Black people in inner city identify with Black people in inner city.

"Growing up, I thought everything was perfect, [even though] I was living a life that was day-to-day survival. It was only the here and now. There were no future goals. [Survival] was about what I was going to eat and do for the day, and I didn't realize it was about the streets I lived on. My life became about surviving violence around me, in the neighborhood, in my home, and in school. I had allowed the things happening in my life to be normalized in a way where it severely traumatized me later on. Becoming an adult [I] understood, 'Wait a minute. That's not okay,' but you don't have a choice when you grow up in the inner city. You have to live by the rules of the streets. In urban communities, there is poverty, there are drugs, there is 'lack of', so there's a higher unemployment rate.

So many families are struggling. There's a lot of unhealthy decision-making that happens by young people and adults, to survive. If we really want to resolve the issues, then we need to focus on the real problems. Not that people are selling drugs, but why do they have to sell drugs? Not that, people have to sell their bodies and prostitute, but why do they have to do that?

We're the most resilient people because we experience violence and witness it day-to-day in some inner cities, and week to week in others. I mean, to be able to survive and overcome and still be successful as an adult…that's HUGE. And people don't look at that. The trauma faced in urban communities is so unique. Some of these [inner city/urban community] situations have been set up by those in power. [They] have set up neighborhoods with lack of access to education, resources, and jobs. And so, to a certain extent, we have caused this. Now we're sitting back and labeling people, and criminalizing the behavior continuously, and still not providing them with the necessary [resources].

[For example…] criminalizing small things—like breach of peace because somebody's arguing. There's a high stress level [in these communities] and you're supposed to be happy and chipper all day? No.

I went from a very innocent, quiet, shy young girl (which people don't believe, but I was), into a very angry, violent teenager. I was fighting all the time, arguing all the time. I turned to some of the normalized coping skills that those in urban community's use: like marijuana, drinking, partying, or skipping school. But even while I skipped school, I still felt my education was very important, so I still made sure that I read. But it felt like I had to do it in secret, because there's a reputation, and you can't be perceived as *weak* in the streets. Because then people will prey on you, take advantage of your kindness and victimize you. So, I had to be tough. And you grow up feeling like everybody is untrustworthy and everybody is out to get you. It's an all-or-nothing mentality. It's a mentality that really takes hold of individuals so strongly, that some people never change that. That stays their norm, even in adulthood." **This is Urban Trauma.**

As examples of how environment impacts day-to-day life, Kyisha recalls being nine years old, sitting at the kitchen table with her brother who was five years younger, and her mother. While eating dinner, Kyisha was holding a fork and all of a sudden, her mother grabbed the fork and yelled at her and said, "I told you to hold it correctly!" and then stabbed Kyisha's hand. Because of being a drug user, Kyisha's mother does not remember that incident, or a lot of the things that she did. Those things happened before the Department of Children and Families took Kyisha away from her home and family. There was a lot of abuse and neglect.

Kyisha tells another story. "I was a teenager, and I was homeless, so I was staying with friends and became a part of some little clique or gang. We were all staying in this one apartment. One day we came back from the downtown mall, late. My friend was opening the door and all of a sudden, we get bum rushed from behind and pushed in by two guys in masks with guns. When they pushed us in, we fell, and they were shooting at us. We were able to crawl to safety. Thank goodness they had bad aim. Honestly, none of us got shot, but it was still very traumatizing. But that's what happens in the inner city. I wasn't a violent person. I wasn't a person who was a criminal. I never stole anything. I never tried to harm anybody else. I just tried to survive and protect myself. And when people think of urban communities and community violence, they really think that it's criminals doing it. It's not always the case. It's more than that. It's what we experience in our homes. Or what we're trying to survive and handle in the streets and then school."

Community violence has impacted me but it also has kept my

eyes completely open to what's really going on and being able to describe things and help people look through a different lens; and how we, as a society and community as a whole, are responsible to bring back some restoration to the community. To bring some healing and some possibilities and opportunities that may not exist. People want it, they are desperate for it."

Policing in Black Communities—The Fight for Survival

There has been a recent visible rise in police brutality among Black men and Black youth. The recent ability to capture on video policing crimes against Blacks has changed the face of the hidden suppression techniques that have been used for decades against Black people. Mothers, fathers, children, families, friends, and neighborhoods are all feeling the emotional pain associated with community violence. Extreme anxiety concerning the health and well-being of Black people has become a common reaction. Resources for us to protect each other are limited, which often leads to frustration and anger. Sometimes we blame ourselves for not doing enough, for not protecting our children, our brothers and sisters. As a result, Black parents everywhere may become overprotective or use punitive discipline in response to their child's trauma-related acting out behavior. It is not uncommon for family members' relationships to become strained. The Black community finds itself in a dilemma of having to reassure each other, while coping with their own fears, knowing deep down inside that safety is not guaranteed. Here is a great example of what a father, friend, and colleague faces raising his two Black sons.

Brett grew up in a large, mostly segregated, middle class town in Ohio. He recalls that his first impression of policing and the correctional system came from a local neighborhood newspaper that featured arrested Black men on the front page of the Wednesday paper. The paper illustrated before and after pictures of Black men that had been arrested by the police. The Black community saw how their people were being treated through photos of the brutality endured during the person's arrest. Men, covered with black and blue marks, broken teeth, busted lips, black eyes, and bleeding all over, were featured on the cover of the newspaper each week.

Word of mouth informed the community of what to watch out for in order to be sure you made it home in one piece. If you were arrested and wound up in the police station, avoid that certain elevator, where they would take you for a beat down. Don't get in your car when police surround you—you don't want to get your head blown off for something you "might" be reaching for. If the police pulled you over, or approached you somewhere, swallow your pride and be polite and accommodating. This is what Black parents taught their children at home—how to survive. These same conversations and lessons—Brett noted after talking to his work colleagues—were not held in the homes of White families.

When Brett was pulled over for a traffic violation his sons saw these survival skills firsthand. At the time, Brett told his sons, "I want you to pay attention to how I interact with the police officer because this is how you're gonna do it in your life." Brett's responses to the officer's inquiries for his driver's license and insurance, in addition to his questions about the traffic incident, were all politely responded to with, "Yes, officer," and "Yes, sir." and "Is there anything else you need, sir?"

When it was over, his sons asked, "What was with all the 'yes, officer, thank you, officer stuff?"

Brett responded, "Because I want you to know that's how you're going get home at night when a police officer pulls you over."

"Survival? Our boys don't survive," Brett said. Brett recalled an incident from his youth.

"I remember at twelve some friends of mine broke into the

elementary school. They broke in, they wrote on the chalkboard, they stole soda out of the teacher's lounge. The police were called. When the police came, the boys ran, which is what boys do. The police shot them in the back. One of them died. One of the boys died for breaking into an elementary school and drinking soda!" **This is Urban Trauma.**

Brett also recalled the story of a job he was doing as a cleaner for a bank. He was sixteen, working in a bank off-hours, buffing the floor. It was hot. He had four jobs to do that night. He removed his work shirt and tucked it into his back pocket. He bought a soda from a machine and left it on the teller's window to take sips between mopping and buffing. Suddenly there was a hard knock on the front door. Brett opened the door and saw officers. They asked him to come outside and pushed him against a wall. Because Brett was young and "full of piss and vinegar" Brett answered the officer's questions in the same tone they were being asked. The officer asked Brett, "Do you want to get out of this alive?" The conversation continued with the officer telling Brett that it looked like he was robbing the bank, that Brett set off a silent alarm. It turned out that when Brett put his soda down a silent alarm was triggered. The interaction that followed with Brett being asked for his ID and work information was less heated, but Brett refused to get in the car to get his ID out of the glove box, afraid that he would be shot over a misunderstanding. In the end, the officer got the ID and he was released without further incident.

Brett explains that when fear is stronger than rage, when you know your life depends on it, you learn to suppress the rage—just to get out of the situation alive. Brett said that with all the new technology, camera phones, and social media, a person can survive an incident and regain his pride later by making sure that the inappropriate response from the officer is shared with the community—in some cases reparations are made financially. But the key is to survive. Brett continues to help young people daily learn how to re-channel the anger they feel. "Young people don't have their judgment center working yet," Brett advised. Young men especially have less patience and more hormones to deal with and aren't always able to suppress the instinct to defend themselves, to resist the dehumanization perpetrated by the police. Many young people tend to go with the rage; they act like a lion, defending themselves. The instinct to fight, to not be disrespected, is often uncontrollable. Brett's mission is to teach the Black kids in his community ways to survive the interaction and then get their dignity back later.

It comes as no surprise that many Black youth are being overrepresented as perpetrators of violence and proactive in crime. The late 1980s and early 1990s, brought about an increase in the number of homicides and robberies reportedly committed by adolescents. One such consequence is commonly known as the school-to-prison pipeline. By 1997, this pipeline demonstrated the factors put in place within the education system to facilitate the criminalization and the incarceration of youth (Morris, 2012), particularly with the inclusion of policing schools in urban areas. It is automatically assumed that teachers must keep their eye out on the Black male student because he is either a class clown, a criminal, or a distraction. As a result, Black students have experienced higher levels of expulsion and suspension compared to their classmates of other races. (Wallace, et al., 2008). Many students have been arrested, expelled, sent to alternative schools, or continuously suspended for minor offenses (Boyd, 2009) that occurred either inside OR outside of school (the Gun-Free School Act of 1994). These disciplinary actions pushed students of color out of the classroom and straight into the juvenile justice system. Black children are detained by the state at higher rates than any other children in the nation (Roberts, 2002).

Mass Incarceration: The "New" Slavery

With the introduction of the Thirteenth Amendment came the abolishment of slavery and the introduction of "freedom" to slaves. The Thirteenth Amendment prohibits slavery or involuntary servitude anywhere in the United States or its territories "except as a punishment for crime whereof the party shall have been duly convicted." The Thirteenth Amendment abolished slavery except as a form of punishment for those found guilty of a crime (Raghunath, 2009; Alexander, 2012). This small clause still allowed those with authority to have control over the freedom of Black people. One particular institution that has taken on this new form of slavery is the prison system (Alexander, 2012). The criminal justice system deprives citizens of their liberty by continuously finding ways to keep them imprisoned. Recent studies of the prison system recognize that a majority of inmates are disproportionately of Black and Latino descent. Private prisons are profiting off of the labor of inmates and bargaining with corporations to increase financial gain. As you may have already deduced, Black men are the ones being targeted. In fact, among Black men in eleven different states, at least one in twenty were in prison. The system became a political and economic machine with mandatory minimum sentences, harsh penalties that do not match the crime, and unnecessary stipulations (Gilmore, 2000) and a contemporary attack to keep Black people—especially Black men—enslaved, limiting their freedom, and restricting their rights (Alexander, 2012). Doesn't this sound familiar?

From the beginning of the 1970s through the twentieth century, there was a rapid rise in mass incarceration. The rise included an upward trend fluctuating from a slow rise in incarceration rates to a quick increase. An example of this was in 1995 when the increase was at a slower rate but still steadily climbing to the extent that there were 447 incarcerated for every 100,000 people in the United States, which was 1.4 million by 2008 (Phelps & Pager, 2016). The expansion of prisons and of incarceration varied by state and was spearheaded by state policy-makers who believed that it was the solution to urban violence and crime (Phelps & Pager, 2016). The astronomical rise of incarceration increased to 2.2 million by 2010, which is 25% of the world incarceration rate even with the United States population being 5% of the world (ACLU, 2017). The data shows that one of the reasons for the rise in mass incarceration is attributed to racial inequality and once again America profiting off the backs of Black people (Phelps & Pager, 2016).

Mass incarceration is an $80 billion per year industry (ACLU, 2017). Mass incarceration has caused social exclusion for Blacks, since they are six times more likely than White men to be arrested and incarcerated (McCorkel, 2016). Some of that increase was influenced by the War on Drugs era. The research has demonstrated that as of 2010 the rate of incarceration in the United States was 62% Black, 27% Latino, and 11% White (Guerino, Harrison, & Sabol, 2012). The overrepresentation of incarcerated Blacks results in higher rates of homelessness, racial regression, increase in the educational achievement gap (includes Blacks having a 40% higher school drop-out rate), and other social issues that work against healthy livable wages and productive citizenship upon release. (McCorkel, 2016).

Michelle Alexander said it best, "Any candid observer of American racial history must acknowledge that racism is highly adaptable. The rules and reason that political systems employ to enforce status relationship of any kind, including racial hierarchy, evolve and change as they are challenged. The valiant efforts to abolish slavery and Jim Crow and to achieve greater racial equality have brought about significant changes in the legal framework of

American society, new rules of the game, so to speak. These new rules have been justified by the rhetoric, new language, and new social census, while producing many of the same results."

Alexander goes on to say, "Since the nation's founding, African Americans repeatedly have been controlled through institutions such as slavery and Jim Crow which appear to die, but then are reborn again in new form, tailored to the needs and constraints of the time. Following the collapse of each system of control, there has been a period of confusion-transition, in which those who are most committed to racial hierarchy search for new means to achieve their goal within rules of the game as currently identified."

The words of Michelle Alexander in 2012 predicted what was bound to happen in November 2016, with the election of the forty-fifth president. Not because she is psychic, but because she understands that history is a cycle of review, revise, repeat. She has intelligently used history to predict and inform future events that are coming to fruition before our very eyes, as we (at times continually) sit in disbelief.

Educational Disparities

Brown v. Board of Education

Limiting exposure to education was one of the decisive tools used during slavery to keep Black people enslaved both physically and mentally. Post slavery, Jim Crow laws prohibited Blacks from sharing schools, restaurants, churches, and other public spaces with Whites. The rise of the NAACP led to many individuals coming together to challenge the protocols put in place. Prior to the Civil Rights movement, segregation was the standard for everything from restaurants to education. These protests and gentle pushback led to the 1896 *Plessy v. Ferguson* case in which separate facilities were fine as long as the facilities were of equal value. However, it was quickly noticed that separate generally did not mean equal.

In 1951, a class action suit was filed against the Board of Education of the City of Topeka, Kansas, in the US District Court of Kansas (*Brown v. Board of Education*). The plaintiffs were thirteen parents on behalf of their twenty children. On May 17, 1954, the court ruled that public schools can no longer separate Black and White students. It was declared unconstitutional for segregation to exist anywhere in the school system. Following this public decree, many public schools struggled to sustain education reformation to challenge segregation in the school system. Court-ordered desegregation started the rapid decline in the separation of students (Guryan, 2004). However, despite federal civil rights laws and public enforcement, progress to integrate equal education opportunities for all students was resisted daily. Although this decision was established in order to implement integration and racial equality, there is still an education gap in existence that isolates students by race and class (Chemerinsky, 2002).

Three years after segregation was announced as unconstitutional, nine adolescent Black youth were given the opportunity to attend a formerly all-White public school. On September 4, 1957, they were escorted by the National Guard and sent into their first day of school. They were greeted with disrespect, profanity, and hostility (Guryan, 2004). Throughout the integration period, Black students would have to endure harassment, violence, and ridicule. Even with efforts to improve equality of education for students of color including low achievement, and poor graduation rates, segregation continued to ensue (Orfield, 1993). Those who did not support the integration within public school systems either fought relentlessly against it or moved their children from public to private school.

Initially, private schools were established due to a preference for religious teachings, better education, and opportunities for students (Saporito, 2003). However, during the late 1950s there was an increase in the number of students enrolled in private and Catholic schools following the Brown decision (Saporito, 2003). Subsequent to the Supreme Court decision, many with high socioeconomic standing, having found the idea of mixing Black and White students offensive, were more likely to pull their children from the local public school and either move or enroll them into private sector schooling. Many White parents found integration of Black students into the private school environment was more difficult due to financial constraints and transportation. Therefore, these private schools were not racially integrated for quite some time. This was known as the "White flight," the movement of White families to districts or schools with fewer Blacks, in order to avoid racially integrated schools.

Simply put, many schools are still separate and unequal despite the court's ruling to create education equality. This fight for school justice and desegregation has in some ways failed students and their families. By any measure, at present, predominantly diverse schools are not equal in their resources or their quality. In a recent study by the education law center, education costs and funding is hindered due to decentralization and concentrated poverty (Baker, Sciarra & Farrie, 2010). The public education system in these areas is full of students either below the poverty line, in poverty, or of low income. In 2011, the U.S. Census stated that nationally, 16% of students attending public school were in poverty. Wealthy suburban school districts are almost exclusively White; poor, inner city schools are often exclusively comprised of Black and Latino students. There is a low expectation for students enrolled in schools located in urban or inner city settings. Inequality goes past skin tone; it also includes the student's socioeconomic status. Therefore, inner city schools face isolation from not only their suburban counterparts, but from private and/or parochial schools as well. This is primarily due to the fact that, in most states, education is substantially funded by local property taxes. Wealthier suburbs have significantly larger tax bases than poor inner cities, and often fewer students to educate. The result is that suburbs can tax at a lower rate and still have a great deal more to spend on education than their inner city counterparts.

Zero Tolerance: A School-to-Prison Pipeline

The zero tolerance policy was put in place to help change the behavior of students. Within this policy, in many school districts, school officials have the option of suspending or expelling students for breaking the rules on school property. Therefore, harsh punishments can be applied regardless of the circumstance. This policy was put in place as an act of prevention around the early twentieth century due to the increase in school violence and school shootings. This policy would allow for minor incidents to receive harsh punishments and consequences that appeared to be out of proportion to the "crime" (Skiba & Knesting, 2001). In a report titled *Violence and Discipline Problems in U.S. Public Schools 1996-1997,* the National Center for Education Statistics (NCES) reported that a majority of school suspensions were a result of minor incidents that did not threaten school safety. For middle school students, the most common factors that led to students being removed from school were disrespect, disobedience, and defiant behavior—in other words, normal adolescent behavior (Skiba & Peterson, 1999). Furthermore, those results illustrated that the majority of the students who were at risk of violating the zero tolerance policy rule were Black and poor. Policies such as this one encouraged the school administration to utilize harsh tactics that result in suspensions, expulsions, and dropouts. School officials were integrating police officers to stop, search, and arrest schoolchildren on, as well as, off school property. Metal detectors were inserted in school, and children are now searched upon entering the building. What was initially implemented for safety would be used to send kids from school to prison. This school-to-prison pipeline drove students into a pathway that begins in school and ends in the criminal justice system. As a result, as reported by a recent U.S. Department of Education study, more than 70% of students arrested in school-related incidents or referred to law enforcement are disproportionately minorities (McNeal & Dunbar, 2010).

So many Black children struggle in school. In particular, Black boys, often as young as two to three years old, are seen as dangerous. Can you imagine that you are a preschool boy behaving as you should, given your age and developmental level, but everything you do—all of your actions and behaviors are scrutinized and viewed as a potential threat. A Yale colleague, Walter Gilliam, PhD, collected data that supports this notion. In Dr. Gilliam's study, he showed that Black preschoolers are 3.6 times more likely to receive one or more suspensions relative to their White counterparts. To put this in perspective, only 19% of preschoolers are Black, but make up 47% of one or more suspensions. This rate is further highlighted as boys are three times more likely than girls to be suspended one or more times. His research sought to explain why.

In his research, Dr. Gilliam developed two tasks for educators (e.g., classroom teachers, student teachers, center directors, and other classroom staff) in various academic levels of preschool. Educators were mostly female and mostly non-Hispanic Whites, who worked in a variety of settings and across student income levels. The two tasks included tracking the eye movements of teachers while watching a video of children in a classroom doing traditional activities and with no challenging behavior. The second task included educators reading vignettes of challenging behavior while varying the student's name to imply differences in gender and race. Background information on the child, or lack thereof, varied as well.

Findings showed several things. First, Blacks—especially Black boys—were watched more when challenging behaviors were expected (although no challenging behaviors occurred in the video). This pattern may imply differing expectations and may explain greater identification of challenging behaviors in real classroom settings for Black boys, even in the absence of such behaviors. The second finding was that the race of the educator was also a determining factor, as was the presence of contextual background information. White teachers lowered behavioral standards for Black students when they had contextual background information; they changed their expectations based on the race of the child (shifting standards theory). However, they also tended to report increased severity in behavioral ratings. Dr. Gilliam's study illustrates that from preschool, Black boys are profiled by their teachers and seen as a potential threat, even in the absence of confirmatory behavior. Based on these assumptions White teachers will rate the severity of behavior far worse than it really is. **A preschool-to-prison pipeline?** You decide.

What is the difference between a White teacher engaging in racial bias and a White police officer racially profiling? In fact, the more complex issue to address is that our Black boys as young as two to three years old are immediately identified as a threat. The truth is that achievement differences are unequivocally tied to race and racism. These are the facts.

In her 2006 book, *Other People's Children: Cultural Conflict in the Classroom,* Lisa Delpit addresses the challenges that educators face concerning the accommodation of multicultural students of ethnic and racial diversity. The author explores the topics of the cultural clash between students and school, stereotyping, teacher assumptions about deficits in diverse children, lowering expectation standards by teaching less instead of more, lack of information about community norms, invisibility, and addressing the problems of educating poor and culturally diverse children.

In the 2007, book *Courageous Conversations about Race: A Field Guide for Achieving Equity in Schools*, authors Glenn Singleton and Curtis Linton conclude that it is not an achievement gap that is keeping Black and Latino children lagging behind in school. Instead, the authors proclaim that institutionalized racism is directly tied to the achievement of students across class lines. Singleton and Linton therefore explore the reality that students of color can no longer afford to have ineffective strategies to address the issues of race. The authors argue that it is unacceptable for teachers not to discuss issues of race, racism, and privilege and it is their responsibility to align with anti-racism teaching strategies. Once racial awareness occurs, conversations to tackle educational disparities in student academic achievement must be addressed in order to challenge the racial consciousness of teachers, staff, and school administrators. To clarify the point, the authors refer to standardized test data to disclose more than an achievement gap based on student ability, but rather a racial achievement gap aggregated by the racial identities of students of color, all scoring significantly below White students. Both of these books are pivotal in addressing the racial achievement gap.

Abolishing the Achievement Gap

In light of lowered educational standards and lack of academic support, many Black adolescent boys and girls are often not prepared to handle the workload in high school and are typically lagging behind compared to their White and Asian counterparts. In the New Haven school district, the District Performance Index (English) was 53.5 Black; 78.2 Asian; 69.9 White. My practice consults with the public school system here in New Haven. Together we have developed this innovative program called Reading Advancement Program (RAP). We created this program as a collaborative effort between the Youth Department in the city of New Haven, the Board of Education, and Integrated Wellness Group. The purpose of the program was to implement a culturally sensitive program that increased reading levels among high school students who were falling in the second- or third-grade reading level, despite their high school status of sophomore, juniors, and seniors (some who are over-aged, under-credited students). RAP is unique in that it is not just a reading program, it also includes social emotional learning (mental health supports) in order to address behavioral or emotional problems that often get in the way of learning. We therefore combined advancing students on their reading levels by using the same reading program applied in school, but with a specialized reading teacher and having a therapist on-site to manage any behavioral problems that may arise. We initially intended for the students to attend the program after school. However, after a small pilot we realized that they were not learning during the school day, so by the time they got to the after school program they were completely frustrated, aggressive, and not open to additional learning. As a result, this year we implemented the program during the school day, as a class period. During the pilot we observed success in: student engagement, steady increase in reading levels, and higher graduation rates. Below are the objectives of the program:

- To meet the educational needs of low-achieving children in school;
- To help close the racial achievement gap between high- and low-performing children, especially the achievement gaps

between minority and non-minority students, and between disadvantaged children and their more advantaged peers;

- To provide the students with an enriched and accelerated reading program that increases self-confidence, self-worth, and self-pride;

- Tutoring, mentoring and other wraparound mental health support structures (therapeutic treatment, assessment, etc.) can support the disadvantaged youth by providing a holistic program for future success; and

- Following a culturally informed community-based support/ intervention, students will successfully re-engage at school to continue making academic gains.

The pilot results: All students identified as Black or African American. All students qualified for free lunch, and most lived in high crime neighborhoods. All students reported having a trauma history (i.e., victim of a violent crime, had a friend die, witnessed shooting, etc.) After the individualized reading intervention and culturally informed mental health supports were put in place, the majority of students increased their reading Lexile per intervention module. Preliminary results suggest that when you provide the right supports in school, Black children—even those who live in poverty, struggle with Urban Trauma, and are academically behind—can still achieve to their fullest potential.

A Face of Urban Trauma in the Classroom: Lisa

The stigmas associated with mental health trickles down into the school system. Besides not having the proper staffing to educate urban youth, the educational system additionally lacks the resources needed to promote mental health assistance. Many mental and physical health concerns with students of color are often not addressed. Few schools have established protocols and procedures that take care of urban youth. Students who show emotional distress, misbehavior, or learning problems are assigned psychiatric labels that often do not match up to their behaviors or life situation. Behaviors are sometimes "diagnosed" by teachers, who lack expertise in this area. This has the potential to lead to misclassification and unnecessary expensive treatments that the Black community cannot afford (Adelman & Taylor, 2006). Activities related to psychosocial and mental health concerns in urban school districts are not often assigned a high priority. Furthermore, despite access to evidence-based interventions, the implementation of interventions and practices do not occur, or if they occur, implementation is fragmented and lacks consistency (Reinke, Stormont, Herman, Puri & Goel, 2011). There is a general lack of cultural competence, even in schools that have school-based clinics. Many teachers feel incapable of managing challenging behaviors in the classroom, utilizing effective classroom management, and/or implementing behavioral strategies (Adelman & Taylor, 2006). In order for progress to be made, comprehensive, multifaceted, and integrated approaches for addressing barriers to mental health need to be implemented (Atkins, et al., 2010). The school system must provide caring and supportive strength-based programs to address the well-being of students.

Lisa's story helps to illustrate the difficulties of teachers trying to manage Urban Trauma. Finding herself at a crossroad on what to do with her life, Lisa wanted to do something meaningful that would allow her to work with children and make an impact on their lives. The obvious answer was to become a teacher. Lisa has a passion for health and physical education and used that as an entry into the school system. Lisa has worked at a college preparatory school in Brooklyn, for the last nine years. Her impressions of the school system are based on this one school in this very urban community.

Lisa has daily contact with the students as their physical education teacher, but she also functions as their advisor. As an advisor, her interactions with students is non-academic, and involves working with them in an informal setting, at a leisurely pace, on planning for fundraisers, school events, and activities. As such, she feels that she has a "pretty good day-to-day relationship with the students in a less academic way than most teachers would have. I think they relax around me because I don't test them," she laughs.

Every day is a challenge for the urban students at her school. In addition to their academic studies, most of them—up to 75% of them says Lisa—have to deal with a mixed bag of emotional and physical issues. Teachers are called upon to be more than educators. Teachers have become role models, substitute parents, guidance counselors, and therapists, and they provide support in whatever form the students need.

One of her first experiences at the school was with a student who lost her brother to gang violence. Lisa observed the siblings interact at one of the school dances and saw that the two had a really good relationship. When this student lost her brother and best friend, Lisa became emotional thinking about how hard it was for this young lady. And the way the brother died and how he was found dead on the street, was particularly heartbreaking. At the funeral, Lisa couldn't imagine how she would've dealt with losing either of her brothers at the age of sixteen.

Another recent incident Lisa recalls was the principal telling a story about a junior, sixteen years old, hospitalized with a sickle cell episode. The principal said, "The parents left her at the hospital and went to Las Vegas!" This news brought Lisa close to tears. "How can a parent leave a child sick in a hospital to go to Vegas?" she exclaimed with disbelief.

In addition to the physical issues of gang violence and illnesses in urban communities, numerous students have emotional distress, academic problems, and behavioral challenges. Many of the students can't read. For example, Lisa described, some of the students come from the Caribbean with low reading levels. The result is behavioral difficulties that affect the ability to teach and for the students to learn. "It does take teachers like me that have those relationships with kids" to keep the kids from succumbing to the pulls of the community—drugs, criminal activities, violence, etc.

Lisa elaborates that school becomes a safe place for children, they have a person to turn to, someone to confide in from outside the home (where sometimes they have to put on strong face), the school becomes a second home. "In our school, we have created a culture where we literally have to kick the students out of the building at 6 p.m. because the kids feel so comfortable there." The children can find someone to talk to and confide in, outside their "messed up" homes. Lisa goes on to tell how most teachers who teach in urban communities are not equipped at all to deal with everything they face each day because of the abundance of [Urban Trauma]. In a group of ten kids, at least seven are emotionally dysregulated. These young people need guidance counselors, social workers, and psychologist. In this school, there are two counselors—each one cares for 150 children! When at least 75 to 80% have psychological trauma that need to be dealt with, and crises are happening daily in school, the staff just can't handle it all. It becomes overwhelming to be a teacher.

Not too long ago, there was a child who lost a very good friend (also to violent crime). Many of the staff knew that this young man was going to explode, but they allowed him to just go on through his day, checking in with him, listening to him say, "Yes, I'm fine." Later that day the student punched out a teacher and got into a gang fight outside of school. If they had given him proper support, the faculty could have prevented all that from happening to the troubled youth. Lisa insists that instead of criminalizing the young man and causing him to act out, teachers should be trained to deal with this kind of situation to avoid that kind of reaction.

As evidence, Lisa relates that earlier this year a seventh-grade, twelve-year-old boy was handcuffed and arrested by police. The principal was heartbroken because she couldn't do anything and the child was basically a good kid. Rules are being changed, trying to make some behaviors unclassified as criminal, but currently the school-to-prison pipeline is indeed very real in schools. **This is Urban Trauma.**

The belief among academics is that this kind of criminalizing is happening more in Black communities than anywhere else. There are zero tolerance rules where teachers and administrators have no choice but to come down hard on the students that act out. Optimistically Lisa hopes that the new school chancellor in New York will affect change by removing punitive punishments and open opportunities for restorative circles, conversations with fellow students, and building a supportive peer group of students in troubled urban communities.

"Support from my parents got me to where I am," says Lisa. A lot of parents have economic disparities and the support is not there for their kids. "Over the years, the number of parents attending our Parent/Teacher conferences has decreased significantly. This lack of parental involvement affects the academic results of students and the behaviors they exhibit in school." Lisa is hoping that in the improvement process, they will focus a larger magnifying glass on inner city schools and the issues that teachers and administrators contend with daily. "They benchmark academics but they are not considering the role of trauma as an obstacle that teachers face in achieving those benchmarks." Mental health and academics can't be separated anymore; they need to be coordinated to achieve greater success for the young people we are educating in urban communities.

After speaking with Lisa, I was interested to see if some of the problems she identified continued into postsecondary settings. I contacted my dear friend and colleague, Dr. Michell Tollinchi-Michel, who has worked as a college administrator for over eighteen years. Dr. Tollinchi-Michel had this to say, "Postsecondary preparation obviously varies from student to student. Students are expected to be very autonomous at the college level and a subset of Black students may find themselves lost because they are not able to make decisions on their own and in turn do not know how to ask for help; they are afraid and embarrassed to ask for help." Some of them may experience "imposter syndrome," the belief that they do not belong in the college setting and are going to be found out. Black students often see adults as "unapproachable, intimidating, and all-knowing so reaching out to them seems almost arduous." Academic preparation also varies and we often see some Black students struggle with writing and are often under-prepared in math and science.

Dr. Tollinchi-Michel goes on to explain that many of the students of color she works with are unable to deal with the stress that comes along with being a college student. They have been known to experience emotional breakdowns, anxiety, depression, and engage in self-sabotaging behaviors. There is a lack of college preparation for Black students who come from disenfranchised communities and are first-generation college attendees. They have limited access to a college environment and the expectations and demands. Dr. Tollinchi-Michel reports that she herself was a first-generation college student, which is what sparked her interest in going into academia. She wanted to help students who faced similar situations, have access to college and she is invested in supporting their success. At the college level, there is limited support around mental health. Many students who come from urban communities may be suffering from Urban Trauma that has not been dealt with appropriately.

PART II

Section One: Urban Trauma Defined

Slavery—The Roots of Urban Trauma

Urban Trauma, first and foremost, is intrinsically linked to multigenerational, historical, and race-specific trauma which can be traced back to slavery.

In 2005, the brilliant author Joy DeGruy contextualized for the world what it has meant for Blacks in America to exist for generations with the legacy of trauma as a result of slavery. She posits that many of the dysfunctions that exist in Black communities (poverty, abuse, mass incarceration, unsuccessful parenting, community violence, and educational achievement gap) can be linked to the crimes committed against our ancestors. In truth, they are manifestations of what she coined to be "Post Traumatic Slave Syndrome." Dr. DeGruy states, "Post Traumatic Slave Syndrome (PTSS) is a condition that exists when a population has experienced multigenerational trauma resulting from centuries of slavery and continues to experience oppression and institutionalized racism today. Added to this condition is the belief (real or imagined) that the benefits of the society in which they live are not accessible to them."

Dr. DeGruy feels it can be simply explained as:

> Multigenerational trauma together
> with continued oppression
> +
> Absence of opportunity to access the
> benefits available in the society
> =
> Post Traumatic Slave Syndrome ... **M+A=P**

Lastly, Dr. DeGruy positions that given the circumstances that produce PTSS, several patterns of behaviors can be identified as directly resulting from chattel slavery.

> **Chattel slavery** is the kind of slavery that existed in the United States before the Civil War. It was legal and historically existed in many parts of the world. Slaves were actual property who could be bought, sold, traded, or inherited.

She identified three categories: Vacant Esteem, Ever-Present Anger, and Racist Socialization. Within all three of these categories, Dr. DeGruy provides examples of common dysfunctional behaviors demonstrated in the Black community.

It was important to highlight Dr. DeGruy's work for several reasons. First, as Black people it is so important to pay homage to those who trailblazed the path of opportunity and understanding for future generations. My quiet admiration for her courage to write such a powerful book knows no bounds. Second, her book beautifully provides the framework for understanding Urban Trauma, in that her work clearly outlines that over 500 years of physical, psychological, and spiritual torture ("180 years of the Middle Passage; 246 years of slavery rape and abuse; and 100 years of illusionary freedom. Black codes, convict leasing, Jim Crow, all codified by our national institutions. Lynching, medical experimentation, redlining, disenfranchisement, grossly unequal treatment in almost every aspect of our society, brutality at the hands of those charged with protecting and serving. Being undesirable strangers in the only land we know") have left their mark on the psyche of Black people and the result has been a legacy of significant trauma.

Urban Trauma allows for an identification and understanding that there is a legacy of trauma or M+A=P (remember this includes oppression and lack of opportunity) experienced by many in the Black community who witness or experience traumatic events but are able to seemingly function in day-to-day life with or without the realization that anything is particularly wrong or meeting any clinical threshold of PTSD.

Like pain, traumatic experiences are filtered through the mind (trying to make sense of it logically) and emotions (feelings of shame, despair, desperation) before it can be considered a debilitating threat. Because of individual differences in how we judge threat, different people appear to have different trauma levels. In some circumstances, individuals will create a more protected layer—what I am calling survival mode—while others are more vulnerable to developing clinical symptoms of PTSD.

Interestingly, while I have been doing this work for years and collecting information one case study at a time, I wish I had known about PTSS much sooner. Despite the fact that Dr. DeGruy's book was published in 2005, over twelve years ago, I did not pick it up until I started to do the research for my own book. I've wondered if I had this framework earlier would I have thought of myself as different, complicated, needy, or aberrant? It is possible that I would have found some sense of normalcy in the definition provided by Dr. DeGruy for PTSS.

As life would have it, the concept of Urban Trauma has been percolating in my head since I started working in urban communities that are generally considered the outliers of society. On my own I was trying to put the pieces together to create definition around not only what happened in my life but also what is happening in the lives of people I am counseling daily. I knew that our history was tied to the way we function today and PTSS has connected the dots for that precise linkage. Now, I am able to build on the framework of PTSS and create a modern-day definition for many urban folks who experience multigenerational trauma, to better understand their psychological state.

Why is this so important you may ask? Well, it was clear the deeper I got into this work that urban and inner city communities are often seen as a troubled, chaotic, dangerous, violent, and as a result, at times, forsaken. Based on my values, I have a responsibility to provide insight into the interconnectedness of our past slavery experience and the present-day status of those who might feel lost, confused, or broken by their current psychological situation. It is my moral imperative to create choice for mental and emotional wellness based on this new level of awareness. Ultimately, my hope is that all those who suffer with Urban Trauma engage in their own healing journey.

A Face of Urban Trauma: Tony

Allow me to introduce you to Tony. Tony helped me grow up as a therapist. He challenged everything I learned in school and threw it out the window. No amount of therapy worked for him. I tried every type of evidence-based treatment out there, and Tony was not getting any better. Instead, sometimes he got worse. One day I told Tony I was all out of ideas. I had nothing left to give him and that maybe I was not the right therapist for him. In turn, he told me,

"Just keep being there, that is enough." Tony changed me, and every aspect of my work.

If Tony's life was like a movie, it would be titled *Urban Trauma*. Tony grew up in a tough inner city neighborhood. His father abandoned him, his mother was a prisoner to a life of drugs, gangs, and crime. Drugs went in and out the house—both for use and for sale. No one had time to think of anything more than the essentials of life: food, clothing, shelter. For a young boy, survival was the game.

While Tony felt at home in his neighborhood, he was often fearful about what could happen to him walking to and from school. He often thought about whether he would be killed, or, "If I fall asleep, someone might stab me or steal my things. If I go outside I could easily get shot for no reason. I will probably not live past the age of 18." HE feared the past, present, and future because everything was so unpredictable. Solidarity and brotherhood with other people sharing your life experiences was natural; loyalty to the people that have your back, inevitable when survival is all you can manage.

In his neighborhood, to survive you had to get along with the people who lived there. (Remember, the historical and family component here, in most circumstances those who experience Urban Trauma are the product of their environment, the same way the children of slaves were the product of the generation before them). So, Tony gravitated to the same life as his parents and the people around him because that was the way you assimilated and stayed out of the line of fire. Don't get noticed. Don't be different. Be tough and aggressive so people won't mess with you.

Tony longed to be noticed by his family. In his reality, he was abandoned; at first emotionally, then by his father when he was incarcerated; then again when he was eight years old, literally, as Tony was taken from the only home and mother he knew and put in "the system." Hoping that the system would provide him with a new home and the attention he needed to stop the cycle of drugs, gang violence, and abuse, Tony was separated from his siblings and placed with a foster family.

In foster care, Tony got the basics: a roof over his head, food to eat, and clothing on his back. Once a child gets into the system, it's hard to pull them out. Where do they discover the motivation to succeed; to study and use education to help them thrive and find their passion? Sometimes foster parents inspire, sometimes they don't.

Due to his aggressive behavior, Tony was medicated and spent his time in and out of psychiatric hospitals. His aggression got the best of him. His anger and all that happened to him was hard to control. His defenses against a society that he felt oppressed him manifested in mistrust and despair. This is Urban Trauma.

When you hear Tony's story and you apply the definition provided, does this sound like a familiar story? Like someone you have treated, educated, or mentored?

What difference did engaging in illegal activities make? Tony learned to manipulate situations and people so that he could get through each day. For a kid like Tony, life on the streets was short. Urban Trauma can take a toll on your mind, body, and spirit. There are times when you will feel broken by all that you have had to endure and you see no way out of your circumstances. Tony's case is severe but not uncommon, especially in urban communities.

The Characteristics of Urban Trauma

Many people with Urban Trauma develop coping mechanisms to get through each day. Race plays a role in developing coping mechanisms as a way to manage additional insults of oppression, racial disparities, microaggressions/unconscious bias, and historical dehumanization.

Microaggressions have been defined as "a statement or action, or incident regarded as an instance of indirect, subtle, or unintentional discrimination against members of a marginalized group such as a racial or ethnic minority."

Implicit or **unconscious bias** has been defined as "the implicit associations we harbor in our subconscious cause us to have feelings and attitudes about other people based on characteristics such as race, ethnicity, age, and appearance. These associations develop over the course of a lifetime beginning at a very early age through exposure to direct and indirect messages. In addition to early life experiences, the media and news programming are often-cited origins of implicit associations." (Willis, T., 2015)

In each characteristic of Urban Trauma, there will exist many features that in isolation are applicable to anyone. However, the collection of these characteristics—understood through a historical and racial lens—create the cornerstone of Urban Trauma. These characteristics then progress in one of two ways: developing a survival mode or, in severe cases, a state of hopelessness and despair. But most importantly, the exploration of each characteristic will illustrate how those with Urban Trauma are often misunderstood, judged, and sometime punished for their affliction. How many with Urban Trauma do not realize they have been traumatized? Do they unknowingly blame themselves, others, or the system for their circumstances? By truly understanding these characteristics, professionals can help those with Urban Trauma link their current stress to generations of traumatic experiences endured by their ancestors. Then they can begin the journey toward healing.

Anger: An Urban Trauma Characteristic

Most Black people in America can identify with the rawest emotion: anger. Consciously or unconsciously, the majority of those with Urban Trauma will identify with anger because there is a deep-rooted resentment that is always present when isolated situations remind us of the almost 500 years of dehumanization, brutality, oppression, and persecution Black people have had to withstand. It is worth reiterating that some may be fully aware of their anger, while others may not recognize that their anger is directly linked to historical oppression and slavery. Yet there are others who firmly believe they are not angry at all.

In a person with Urban Trauma, anger may quickly surface from the unconscious to the conscious level when an incident occurs that feels all too similar to acts of historical racial discrimination. Consider how those with Urban Trauma may feel when they watch one of their own being beaten or brutalized by a White police officer. Anger will be the most common <u>initial</u> emotion that is triggered when such situations are witnessed.

From my experience, anger comes in three forms.

- <u>Overt/Aggressive Anger.</u> The in-your-face and most obvious type. It is the reaction that looks like you are flaring up, becoming defensive, sometimes combative, verbally aggressive, and physically worked up. To give a few examples, overt anger can surface when faced with microaggressions; for instance, when you are shopping at a store and being followed, or when you are profiled for no other reason than because you are driving while Black. The anger that results from Urban Trauma may seem way too intense to fit the situation, but the reality is that it is always percolating beneath the surface, just like a volcano ready to erupt. Once the circumstance aligns with the emotional reaction, it takes seconds for that anger to well up and come out, in behaviors that at times seem out of control. There are a number of situations (so many that it would change the focus of the book) that I can describe to solidify the rage that weaves in and out of urban Black communities daily.

- Anger Through Sarcasm. Many people use sarcasm as a way to unload their anger. Over the years, sarcasm, in my opinion, has become a strategy developed as a subtler response when in conflict. For many, sarcasm is an ideal way to manage White folks, because you are able to "check" them without resorting to overt or inward anger. Sarcasm is at times masked by humor or a verbal jab slipped into a conversation—it is quick and unassuming. It is also a masterful way to disguise defensiveness or denial. Sarcasm can be used as a deflection strategy—most people who are on the receiving end of sarcasm will most likely shift their focus to the sarcastic statement directed toward them, rather than remain focused on the initial reason for the conversation. This is the art of deflection.

- Anger Turned Inward. This is the type of anger that includes being self-destructive, depressed, and sabotaging yourself. It's the one that is rooted in insecurities. Those experiencing Urban Trauma may retreat or shut down. When you ask, "What is wrong?" They may say, "Nothing." But it is clear that something is not quite right. In my opinion, anger turned inward is the most dangerous, particularly since the anger is not being demonstrated. It is inconspicuous, as if nothing is particularly wrong, but all the while the person is seething inside (sometimes unconsciously), with each incident building resentment and additional anger. Like a pot of boiling water, it is only a matter of time before it boils over.

There are many of us who will relate to one of these three ways of managing anger. Often depending on our personalities, one style feels more comfortable than the other. Likewise, depending on the situation, one style may be more suitable than the other.

Reflection
The question here is not whether a person affected by Urban Trauma will experience anger. That is inevitable. What is really at stake is what will they do with that anger? How can we prevent it from consuming them? What can prevent them from going down a road of self-destruction?

When the Tribe is Under Attack

Picture the reaction of Black men when they saw the video of Trayvon Martin being shot down. Picture Black women's connection to this handsome young man as they saw in Trayvon the face of their son, brother, nephew, cousin, or friend. Consider how some in the Black community felt when a jury rendered a not guilty verdict for Zimmerman—a sobering reminder of the treatment of Black people in America and the value of Black lives. What is the difference between chattel slavery and the current and deliberate persecution of Black boys and men today? Is it just perceived freedom? Has the matrix continued to change in order to provide the illusion of freedom?

My son was fifteen when Trayvon was killed. As any mother would, I worry about my son. But unlike every mother, I worry knowing that he is a young Black teen who is trying to survive in a world that has no love for him. With Trayvon's death the conceptual overreaction response of what could happen collided with a large dose of reality (what did happen). The outcome: I was paralyzed by fear. Trayvon's death brought into question my son's chances of survival in this world—a thought that became all too real. Maybe it was because of the innocence that I saw in Trayvon's face, maybe it was because my son wears hoodies all the time, maybe it was because of their closeness in age, maybe it was because as a psychologist I recognize the fearlessness and sense of invincibility that is so developmentally appropriate for an adolescent since their brains are not fully developed. I understand all too well that insight and maturation emerges much later in boys (sometimes not until age twenty-five or later) and that our Black boys are being handled like grown men by police who have limited or no training in normative adolescent brain development. It was heart-wrenching to see my son leave the house. Every time he left I prayed that it would not be the last time I saw him. I had vivid nightmares about potential situations that could happen to him even during nights that he was home. In my eyes he became an endangered species.

I often ran down to his room in the middle of the night and just watched him sleep. I had a keen sense of hypervigilance. I lived in fear for my son. I saw that he did not worry as much as I did and that worried me even more. I saw that the freedom he thought he had is really not freedom at all. His dad and I sat him down and talked to him about how he should conduct himself if ever stopped by the police. We belabored the point! We contradicted our rearing of him, by telling him that in this situation he did NOT have freedom of speech, because in this situation his life depended on keeping his mouth shut and humbly following the directives of any police officer, whether right or wrong.

In true fashion he highlighted our hypocrisy, but we did not care. This was not a discussion or debate. There was no choice for him, but to follow our rules. Sternly we scolded, "If you are ever stopped, keep both hands on the steering wheel, 'yes, sir' and 'no, sir' is how you will respond, keep your wallet visible so you do not have to reach for your driver's license, make no sudden movements ever, and lastly DO NOT wear hoodies outside of this house! We are not playin'." This was the hardest parenting moment for us, as we knew the statistics: Black men are twice as likely to be stopped, questioned, and criminalized by police. Shoot and ask questions later. Today my son is nineteen years old, a college student and an athlete who has his entire beautiful life ahead of him. We worry as much today, if not more, than we did then. I mourn over Trayvon's tragic death and feel so much sorrow in my heart for his mother. I could never, ever imagine her pain. But I can in many, many ways relate to her anger.

Anger in Black Men

Black men who experience anger as a result of Urban Trauma are immediately characterized as aggressive, violent, and dangerous. This stereotype has supported America's view of Black men as a threat, instead of being viewed and understood through the lens of Urban Trauma.

Throughout our history, society has painted Black men as aggressive, often associated them with criminal-like behavior, and assumed they deserve whatever form of punishment is given because they continue to be subhuman. Even if that punishment means death. If we look at modern-day slavery or what Michelle Alexander terms the New Jim Crow, we are keenly aware that Black men are over-represented in the penal system. "More African Americans are under the control of the criminal justice system today—in prison or jail, on probation or parole—than were enslaved in 1850." Every time I read this statistic, I am impacted as if it was the first time I heard it.

Let that sink in.

The reality is that Black men have been seen as perverse for centuries. Black men are pulled over for questionable reasons more often than Whites or Latinos. They are also more likely to have the deadliest outcomes if they are perceived as uncooperative (meaning not submitting to the law and the authority of police). Nationwide, Black drivers were 31% more likely to be pulled over than Whites, the *Washington Post* reported in 2014. Black drivers were more than twice as likely to be subject to police searches. The Justice Department statistics, based on the Police-Public Contact Survey, reported that 12.8% of Black drivers, 9.8% White, and 10.4% Latino drivers—were pulled over in a traffic stop. These results confirmed that Black drivers are 31% more likely to be pulled over than a White driver and about 23% more likely than a Latino driver.

An analysis based upon stop and frisk data from New York Civil Liberty Union (NCLU) reported that Black and Brown communities continue to be the target of police stops and street interrogation. According to NYPD police reports, nine out of ten individuals who were stopped and frisked have been completely innocent, but are most often Black. Consider this: New York is likely the most liberal state in the country, with a progressive mayor, liberal governor and attorney general, and with many Democrats in power. Yet despite this seemingly liberal political landscape, limited progress has been made to change the culture of

New York law enforcement, police-community relations, and the juvenile justice vortex. In the first three quarters of 2016, New Yorkers were stopped by the police 10,171 times. Of that number, 76% were innocent. The racial breakdown of the stops: 54% Black, 29% Latino and 10% White.

To further explore this idea of anger as a characteristic of Urban Trauma and in particular with Black men, I was having a casual conversation with some friends and this was the outcome of that dialogue.

A Face of Urban Trauma: Shawn

Based on Shawn's life experiences, anger in itself is a very raw emotion. Shawn states, "I think that anger becomes a culmination of different events from your history, events that create a narrative. When anything flicks that irritable vibe, the raw emotion just strikes out. My perception is that anger is not just connected to that moment of disrespect. Anger is connected to the historical way by which Black men have been treated in our society from the day that the first slave was forced here."

Shawn reflects, "I think that the rage that you can feel in a particular scenario connects back to the fact that out of all the things that we've done, all the things that we've accomplished as a people, that for somebody to still even think that they can approach you in that manner, makes you really want to kind of have off with their head. It's not a rational response necessarily but, it's certainly understandable."

With certainty Shawn elaborated, "When you're younger, you have less control over those raw emotion because you're not accustomed or even aware that you need to control it. As you become older, you learn how to control it. The things that make me angry these days are things that I take as a disrespectful or as a personal affront to ME in particular. When somebody basically disrespects me, it's like they're calling into question my manhood, in a sense. White people, sixty years ago even, didn't think that we were men or their equal. That then conjures up emotions. You want to show them that you're a man. And, in showing them, depending on your disposition, can trigger the type of anger where you feel like you need to physically show them by imposing your might on them."

"I don't know that most Black men exist in an angry state," explains Shawn. "I think that most Black men that I know understand that the cards are stacked against you. And I guess sometimes, in that understanding, it can definitely piss you off. However, I think that if you are a Black man that has navigated through society unscathed, then you come to accept it as a part of this game that you've been playing for so many years. I expect him [White men] to be my enemy, then I'm not surprised when he does something evil, or when he tries to do something evil to me.

"I feel the historical rage comes from the standpoint of 'Who the f*#k do you think you are?' and 'What have you done that makes you think that you can approach me with such disdain? What God or deity actually told you that you were better than me?' and so on. THEN, because of my disposition, I'm going to feel like …Let me show you that you're not better than me! Let's go down the line and look at your family, and for me to look at my family, and play with 'That one's not better than this one.' 'I'm better than this one.' 'This one is not better than that one.' Just to completely prove to you beyond a shadow of a doubt, that this falsehood that you possess in your head, about you all being some type of supreme race or just entitled to have this feeling of superiority, is totally utter bull, to be honest. I think, when you're approached with that type of racism, or oppression, you feel anger.

I deal with White people every day, all day, nowadays you experience racism in more of the subtle microaggressions, it has become much more sophisticated. Then, in its subtlety, for you to respond with rage is, in effect, out of place. That type of subtle disrespect becomes like a mental or verbal sparring match, or chess game, which is not a situation into which you would necessarily bring rage. Instead, you use things like sarcasm to deal with your anger and serve subtle but powerful blows when you can."

After this conversation, we both sat in sobering silence. I think that for my friend it was the first time that he actually verbalized his deep-rooted feelings about White men and how they make him feel. It makes one realize how important respect is to Black men no matter their social or economic level and what lengths they will go through to make sure that they are not disrespected.

As I listen to him talk, I thought about the young Black men I work with who are living in a state of Urban Trauma and how often they are disrespected by their teachers, peers, police, and our society in general. I thought about the story of Kalief Browder, who in his documentary *Time: The Kalief Browder Story* (which was filmed before and after he took his life), said when talking about Black kids in the streets of New York City, "Their homes are not good, they don't feel loved. Already conditioned. Kids in urban America don't have the right to be human." Kalief, at the tender age of sixteen, was wrongly accused of stealing a backpack. He was arrested and placed in Riker's Island Prison to await trial. His mother did not have the money to post the $3,000 bail that was set. As a result, he spent more than one thousand days in prison. Eight hundred of those days were spent in solitary confinement, where he was beaten, abused, starved, and psychologically and mentally tormented. Where was the respect for Kalief? For his life? So of course, Black men have the right to be angry. When we couple justified anger in Black men, with a collection of racial traumas, disrespectful treatment, and demeaning experiences; these emotional states lend themselves to the development of Urban Trauma.

Anger in Black Women

Now, let's talk about anger and Black women. Have you ever heard that term, "Angry Black woman?" Black women have fallen prey to this stereotype. I Googled the term "angry Black woman" to see if there was a descriptor or definition, since the term has become so popular. To my surprise there were pages of information and descriptions of the angry Black woman:

"Angry Black Woman is a derogatory term that refers to Black women."

Anger and Black women have become so intertwined that the terms are assumed to mean the same thing. Stereotypes fuel misconceptions such as "If you are a Black woman, you must be angry." Additionally, it seems as though Black women can either be angry or strong; never both and never something in between (like assertive). Assertiveness by a Black woman will almost always be interpreted as anger.

The connection between Black women, anger, and Urban Trauma was the most difficult topic to address in my research for this book. I have done my best with an incredibly complicated topic—that extends to not only race, but also to gender—to describe what I believe are the issues that connect anger in some Black women to Urban Trauma.

Historically, the Angry Black Woman view stems from a belief that Black women are more expressive, passionate, or verbose. In American culture, depictions of the Angry Black Woman were being portrayed in movies, dance, and film beginning in the early 1900s. It then cultivated a stereotype "grasping on to the belief that Black women are not only expressive, but more opinionated, harsh, have bad attitudes, are loud, and generally negative and rude in nature." (Bennett & Morgan, 2006; Childs, 2005)

Urban Trauma affects Black women at the same rate that it affects Black men. In some cases, it may be worse among women. For instance, young Black girls are forced to mature faster and handle more responsibility at home and in the community. Girls who experience Urban Trauma have had to contend with violence of all types, including sexual, physical, emotional, and psychological. This is in addition to carrying the burden of becoming parentified (taking on adult responsibilities) early on by caring for the household—their mother, father, and siblings. Later they may become the sole provider for their children. Black women are taught to be strong and to carry the burden of their families, neighborhoods, and communities—at the same time they cannot be too strong or they become too masculine, bossy, and run the risk of emasculating their partners.

I sat with a group of sister friends I know very well, in a small intimate setting designed to talk about issues that affect women of color.

One of the women in the group started by saying, "Black women are angry because we feel like our men don't value us. Black men have forgotten how to take care of their families, to put us and their children first. They require too much ego stroking and careful handling. Nobody has time for that, when we work all day, then have to deal with the kids, make dinner, keep the house clean, help with homework, and by the time we are done the last thing we want to think about is them and their needs—what about our needs?" Another woman interjected, "Black women carry the baggage of seeing their mothers and aunts and other women in their family having to suffer with the Black men that they've dealt with. The cheating, lying, anger, and sometimes violence." She went on to say, that she felt her ex "hated on her" for being successful, "I will admittedly say that Black men have failed as fathers and stewards of the Black family. For this reason, it is hard for us to trust. Trust has been broken so many times, we have been disappointed over and over again. Sometimes it's hard for me to smile, because there is simply nothing to smile about."

Another woman in the group exclaimed, "We are always fighting against beauty standards that often do not represent images of us. These beauty standards perpetuate historical colorism and sometimes cause tension between Black females. One could say that the image we've been fed of beauty is not that of a Black woman, and it is a painful reality."

Yet another sister spoke up and said, "It is also important to acknowledge that at times we [Black women] feel we are on an island…all on our own. Think about the feminist movement. Since suffrage we have been left out. So even though we had gender in common, it was not like we could turn to White women for support either."

Look at the results of the 2016 Presidential election. White women overwhelmingly voted for Trump.

These examples alone do not cause Urban Trauma in Black women. However, when the anger begins to teeter into frustration, irritability, confusion, lack of trust, and hostility then we must consider the role that Urban Trauma is playing. Urban Trauma can make people feel like shutting down or can cause disconnectedness or feelings of numbness or of being overwhelmed. Because Black women play such an integral role in the family unit, their Urban Trauma has a lasting ripple effect (see epigenetics section). For this reason, when working with those who experience Urban Trauma it is important to observe the quality of their relationships with their children, friends, peers, partners, and ex-partners. If these relationships are broken, fragmented, or in a constant state of conflict, consider the role of Urban Trauma. Unlike men, I believe that Black women will carry more of the multigenerational trauma with them. Therefore, Urban Trauma for many women can occur without a precipitating event. Given the burden carried by Black women, the matriarchal nature of their role in the Black family and community, and the multigenerational genetic traumatic underpinnings, Urban Trauma can occur without a catalyzing stressful event.

In sum, no matter the gender, in severe cases, anger can go beyond Urban Trauma. When anger becomes explosive, full of rage, characterized by violence, triggered easily and without provocation, or disproportionate to the situation, then we may need to consider a psychiatric disorder. For example, if the person is experiencing heart palpitations, tightening of the chest, increased blood pressure, headaches, tingling in their body, or chronic headaches associated with an angry outburst, this is more critical than Urban Trauma. One should seek medical and/or psychological guidance.

MISTRUST: An Urban Trauma Characteristic

Merriam-Webster's definition of trust is "one in which confidence is placed, assured reliance on the character, ability, strength, or truth of someone or something." Trust when you have endured Urban Trauma is very difficult to accomplish. Trust suggests you would place confidence in someone or something, meaning that they will bring you no harm, that you will be treated fairly, and without judgment.

With Urban Trauma, trusting is very complicated and often difficult to accomplish. Think about this from a historical lens: How has trust developed in the Black community dating back to slavery? Think about trust between Blacks and Whites. And trust within the Black community. Trust has been systematically broken for centuries, and continues to be abused. So how can we ever expect those with Urban Trauma to trust anyone?

In my years of doing this work, I have noticed that for those who have experienced Urban Trauma there are one of two major ways to trust: Trust over Time or Trust Unconditional Until.

Trust over Time suggests that you do not trust anyone, and if you were to trust, it often takes years. Take the example of Jackie who has experienced Urban Trauma. Jackie meets a new colleague and friend at work, Emily. Jackie is usually tentative about the actions and intention of all those around her, including but not limited to, those from her race or community, but is especially tentative about White folks. Trust over Time in the context of Urban Trauma, suggests that there is an initiation process by which Emily must undergo test after test, before Jackie is able to trust her. Emily has no clue that all of her movements are being closely monitored and scrutinized by Jackie in order to determine her trustworthiness. Sometimes the test consists of Jackie sharing small (but often fairly irrelevant) pieces of information just to see what Emily will do with this information. If the information shared never gets back to Jackie, then Emily is one step closer to becoming trustworthy. However, if Emily fails any of the "trust test," she will be handled differently. For Jackie, trust is earned over time, and only as a result of many situations or circumstances by which Emily successfully passes the test. Interestingly, in Urban Trauma passing the test does not guarantee unrestricted trust access. So you must remain consistent if you want to be considered trustworthy.

Within Urban Trauma, the other way to trust is with full investment: Trust Unconditional Until. These folks are an open book, living life freely; they are going to appear to take you as you are.

Take the example of Curtis and Eric. Curtis, who has experienced Urban Trauma, is new to the Maryland area and at a social gathering meets Eric. Curtis considers himself a pretty authentic person, so he handles his friendships the same way. Eric was vetted by a mutual friend so there is a sense of initial trust. On a few occasions, Curtis has asked Eric out for a drink to just chill or hang out. Eric agrees to meet up every time he's invited, but the last three times he has flaked out on Curtis. Last week, Curtis had a flat tire about two miles from Eric's house. He called Eric for help, and waited for over an hour but Eric never showed up (this may trigger other characteristics of Urban Trauma). A week later, Curtis sees Eric at a party, where Eric is telling everyone that Curtis is his "tight boy." What do you think Curtis's reaction is, given his experience with Urban Trauma coupled with his way of trusting? You might say, "Well Curtis trusts unconditionally." Actually, no. In fact, Curtis was watching how Eric manages the trust he has been given. He is testing this friendship. Now Eric has proven a pattern of behavior, that he is flaky and not trustworthy. This friendship in Urban Trauma will not last and Eric will mostly likely be set to the side or cut off all together.

In Urban Trauma, the difference between Trust over Time and Trust Unconditional Until is the approach. In both, you are testing the other person, observing their actions and behaviors, looking for patterns, and watching to see if betrayal is lurking. In both you are wary of intentions, and trying not to have expectations. Placing expectations in relationships where trust is consistently tested can become fairly exhausting. It is important to understand that in

Urban Trauma, relationships have been compromised by let downs, false promises, and disappointments. Because relationships are so fragile within Urban Trauma, these rules must be applied for survival. In Urban Trauma given the experiences with unpredictable relationships, severing them when needed is not very difficult. In many cases you come to accept that most people are not trustworthy. In both, if there is betrayal (or perceived betrayal) that relationship stands a very small chance of survival. An important detail to note with Urban Trauma is that while reminiscing or mourning the loss of the relationship is a normal reaction, so is emotionally severing relationships, sometimes in a callous approach, if trust is violated. To some this may seem antisocial, to me it is perfectly distinctive of Urban Trauma.

In severe cases, such as when you have PTSD, the trust issues move into a realm of complete emotional detachment or emotional numbing. People experiencing this level of symptomatology may also experience dissociative, or depersonalization types of reactions. Some have described it as an out-of-body experience. While they are physically present, emotionally they feel as if they are watching themselves interact with others because their mind is elsewhere. There is a lack of emotional connection. People with this problem often have emotional systems that are in overdrive. They may have a hard time being a loving family member, spouse, or friend. They may avoid activities, places, and people associated with any traumatic events they have experienced. The difference between Urban Trauma and PTSD here is that with Urban Trauma you detach from the relationship because trust has been broken. With PTSD you detach or disconnect from emotions, people, and relationships in order to cope with the past traumatic experiences but also to cope with daily stressors.

Defining PTSD:

Symptoms of PTSD may include nightmares or flashbacks, avoidance of situations that bring back memories of the trauma, hypervigilance, anxiety, or depressed mood.
Behavioral: agitation, irritability, hostility, hypervigilance, self-destructive behavior, or social isolation
Psychological: flashbacks, fear, severe anxiety, or mistrust
Mood: loss of interest or pleasure in activities, guilt, or loneliness
Sleep: insomnia or nightmares
Other associated symptoms: emotional detachment or unwanted thoughts.

MANIPULATION: An Urban Trauma Characteristic

A means to an end. Imagine that your daily reality is that you lack trust and that it is difficult to honor the people who live in your world. When these aspects of our relatedness to people come into question, as they do with Urban Trauma, we don't root relationships in true reciprocity. Instead those experiencing Urban Trauma may see relationships as leverage—as a way to get personal and individual needs met—a means to an end. It is my belief that manipulation is a distortion of relationship-building, rooted in the times of slavery when many Black slaves had to use these tactics in order to survive. Manipulation is very much a survival tactic and therefore, a characteristic of Urban Trauma.

People who have experienced Urban Trauma use soft manipulation skills, such as lying, to control situations. You may witness them embellish, overreact, or remix certain situations, usually for personal gain. They may tell subtle lies that can be confusing, chaotic, or incomplete. The person on the receiving end may feel that they are on a rollercoaster—because it is hard to discern the falsehoods from reality. For the person experiencing Urban Trauma, controlling the information allows for room to manipulate people, relationships, and/or situations further if necessary. They will not elaborate or tell you more than you need to know.

There are other complex interactions that also take place. For instance, it is very difficult for individuals who have experienced Urban Trauma to take personal responsibility or ownership over their behavior. They are accustomed to being a victim, and at times this mentality has helped them get out of very tough situations unscathed. Remember, those with Urban Trauma have been subject to generations of dehumanization as a result of slavery, racism, oppression, poverty, and lack of opportunity. Most are ancestral victims of Jim Crow, housing discrimination, redlining, education disparities, community violence, and police brutality. They enter into a vicious cycle of being abused by the system and then go on to master the system in order to survive.

Manipulation becomes one of the most useful tools in the survival game. If you are good at it, and learn to hustle your way in and out of situations, you have a much higher rate of survival. Manipulation is learned very early on, is easily adaptable among and between cultures, and can be easily harnessed to drive success in any situation. You learn to read people and situations, and anticipate next steps; thereby preparing for future events. You have an innate and intuitive awareness of human behavior, and are able to drive the relationships by the way you maneuver them. You become a relationship master (unfortunately, those "relationships" are mostly superficial). You become a connector by nature, since connecting the dots, people, and situations support your keen sense of survival.

Just like anger and mistrust can progress into more severe conditions, if not controlled, manipulation can escalate into the realm of psychopathology, teetering on sociopathic behavior such as personality challenges, lack of appropriate attachment, and in some cases PTSD.

A Face of Urban Trauma: Jacob

One of my most complicated cases in my years of practice is that of Jacob. He was abandoned at eighteen months by his biological mother and left to fend for himself at this tender age. Jacob was found after several days in an apartment; his mother had left him and a younger sibling so she could go binge on drugs. Jacob was nothing short of angry, and had most certainly experienced Urban Trauma. As a toddler/preschooler he became violent, did not want anyone touching him, and was very sensitive to human interactions. Initially, he found a way to push people away, making sure in his young mind that no one would hurt him that way again.

I have had the pleasure of seeing him grow up over the years. Jacob's developmental stages have not been easy, neither for him nor for his adoptive family. As a preteen, he is very handsome, and I have begun to see how the once student of people has now become a master manipulator. Needless to say, this child's Urban Trauma has extended into the realm of a mental health disorder, however, you can still see core characteristics of Urban Trauma present. This child knows when a person he is interacting with has a weak character. Jacob knows when a person enables behavior, defuses boundaries, avoids conflict, is tentative, vacillates in decision-making and so forth. It is also clear to Jacob when he has encountered a person who sets clear and consistent boundaries, provides love, structure and nurturing discipline, and most—important of all—is not a pushover or cannot be easily manipulated. Jacob is able to discern characteristics and behaviors that most adults are unable to do in their daily interactions with others. In some ways, he is gifted in his study of people. These skills did not develop by chance, they developed by training in an unfortunate set of circumstances. Imagine, however, if these skills are positioned appropriately, Jacob can turn out to be an amazing sales guru; his relationship skills lend themselves to the marketing or advertising field—as he will keenly understand the psychology around purchasing power.

The problem occurs when these characteristics are not harnessed appropriately. People with Urban Trauma need to learn the skills to not just survive, but to thrive in a world that they do not trust, and more often fear (sometimes because they are feared). The first step is to help them understand that it is possible and that they can live loving, trusting, productive lives. But it takes a great deal of emotional work to get there.

FEAR: An Urban Trauma Characteristic

As a result of slavery, Black people were conditioned into fearing Whites through violence, punishment, intimidation, harassment, and a fully waged psychological war. I believe that when White people encountered us those many centuries ago they feared our strength, our sense of collective living, our intelligence, our spiritual connection, our respect for Mother Earth, our familial and tribal customs, and our general kindness and love for humanity. White people were afraid and confused because these were not typical European customs, so they set out to destroy what they did not understand.

I believe that when the first encounter took place, and the first Africans were sold into slavery by tribe members, there were two events happening simultaneously. The Africans who were accustomed to selling rival tribal members into servitude (to demonstrate their conquest over another tribe) could never have imagined the brutality demonstrated during chattel slavery in the Caribbean or the Americas. I also opine that the Europeans themselves did not initially intend to dehumanize Africans—just to conquer them. My conviction is that centuries ago, when fear met greed and power, slavery was given a new face. Fear kept the institution of chattel slavery moving forward. And once money became part of the equation, there was no turning back, even if some Europeans considered the treatment of Africans inhumane. For instance, in 1790 the U.S. held 692,567 enslaved Africans. Translated into dollars we are looking at $5.5 billion in today's value. This legacy rings true today, as there are many Whites that continue to become wealthy off the backs of Black people, some who are professional poverty pimps. The privatization of prisons is just one of many examples.

Today, fear is what has driven most of the assaults against Black people and continues to do so. Fear has created a way of life in communities of color. Fear causes urban communities to function in a reactionary and crisis-driven state. Fear does not allow for thoughtful planning and execution of bettering our communities. Fear is paralyzing and consumes our thinking and stunts action. Urban communities have existed under the constant attack driven by fear. Compare this reality to other cultural or religious communities that have been able to thrive and flourish without fear (of violence, oppression, assault, percussion, racial inequalities, discrimination) hovering like a dark cloud over their very existence.

The Black community has evolved, from slavery to present day, to live in a constant state of fear. This has led to the creation of three manifestations of fear for those who experience Urban Trauma.

1. <u>Fear of failure and fear of success</u>. As an example, let's consider fifth-grader Anne who has Urban Trauma. Many students, like Anne, with Urban Trauma struggle with delays in school. From my observation, school success is not tied to true intellectual ability. Instead it is directly connected to the high level of distress experienced daily in urban communities, thereby interfering with their ability to learn. On the other hand, if you are able to manage the multiple demands of school, home, and community, then there is fear of success. What does success really look like if you are the first in your family to graduate, to go to college, to get a job? Are you truly deserving of the rewards that come along with success? Are you an imposter?

2. <u>Fear of the unknown</u>. Many of those with Urban Trauma rarely leave the perimeters of their neighborhood. The world exists within a ten-block radius. Venturing to other places, experiences, and possibilities are self-restricted. Leaving the neighborhood is often not a top choice for those with Urban Trauma, mostly because of their fear of the unknown.

3. <u>Duplicity.</u> Most people, but in particular those who experience Urban Trauma, have had moments when they

say one thing and do another. Most times, however, those experiencing Urban Trauma exist in multiple states of incongruency. This means that what they say does not align with their intentions, and their intentions do not align with their behavior. We are one way on the inside and another persona on the outside. The outside persona is typically tied to the social expectations placed on us based on how we are perceived. For example, if you were born and raised in the 'hood, you are a Black male, people may automatically assume that you are gang involved, use or sell drugs, or that you are a criminal; perhaps there is an expectation or stereotype that you are a thug, gangsta, or tough guy. If you know this is the societal expectation, do you play the role? Do you live up to the stereotype of a gangsta, regardless of whether you are one or not? do you need to be tough, demonstrate, hardness, perhaps smoke marijuana, listen to a certain type of music, or wear your pants bagged down? But consider that maybe you are very intelligent, actually enjoy learning, and have a great ability to achieve beyond the expectations of the teachers, streets, or even yourself. Do you allow the true you to come out—perhaps the more nerdy you—or do you have to play the role of a street thug? The fear of fighting the odds, confronting the status quo and what is expected takes exceptional courage.

Fear, in severe cases, can move beyond Urban Trauma to enter the realm of psychological conditions that can become quite debilitating. For example, irrational fears exist in the clinical anxiety category. These fears are typically not based in reality, but instead are rooted in perceived threats, or feelings of discouragement or shame. Let's consider people who have panic attacks, which are characterized by sudden and repeated attacks of fear that last for several minutes or longer. These panic attacks are characterized by a fear of disaster or of losing control even when there is no real danger.

PERCEPTION: An Urban Trauma Characteristic

We have all experienced moments when there are two or more people, at the same place at the same time, and everyone leaves with a different version of what happened. We have heard idioms such as, "your perception is your reality."

A host of negative perceptions exist, and have existed, about Black people dating at least back to slavery and very possibly beyond. For example, perceptions related to our intellectual and mental inferiority have been a common place myth that as individuals, and as a community, we have had to challenge. This perception of inferiority was utilized and reinforced by the European's desire to rule over Black people. Based on their perception of warrior vs. slave, they considered Africans docile and easily mastered. Yet based on African customs, there was no need to engage in war for the sole purpose of greed, power, and conquest. In African, and in other indigenous cultures, conquest was not the only solution for expanding tribal footprints. Marriage between tribes, sacrificial gifts, and treaties were more peaceful ways to accomplish the same agenda—without the bloodshed. It is my belief that climate changes faced by Europeans, after their migration from Africa, not only changed the color of their skin, but genetically altered their human interactions to be conquest driven, at times barbaric, and thereby becoming more ruthless and cruel. As a result, the seemingly less evolved African way of life, from the Europeans' perception, was easier to conquer and birthed the notion of Black inferiority. Over time, and as the heinous assaults against Black people worsened, this perception evolved into all categories of Black human existence. Black people were, and many cases still are, considered by Whites:

- Intellectually inferior, despite all of the evidence that we contributed to the creation of math, science, and entire civilizations all over the globe;
- Physically inferior, despite our ability to withstand the power of the sun, given our rich melanin and ability to engage in strenuous hard labor jobs;
- Spiritually inferior, despite our love, honor, respect, and acknowledgment for all that is Godly and tied to Mother Earth;
- Mentally inferior, despite our ability to overcome the most horrendous of circumstances and still we stand.

No matter what we have done as Black people to disprove the myths, over and over and over again, that there is not a single molecule that is inferior, that perception stands true today. The devastating aspect of Black inferiority is not the European perception of us, but that this perception has taken its toll on the Black psyche and that many of us, especially those with Urban Trauma, engage in self-hatred because of our own struggle with Black inferiority.

In order to understand how we, as a community, got here it is important to explain how perceptions are created in the first place. Perception has been defined as "a process of interpretation of a present stimulus [situation] on the basis of past experience." This means there is a great deal of information that we process in order to understand the world around us.

Perception, when defined in conjunction with Urban Trauma, includes perceptual learning, mental sets, motives and needs, and cognitive styles. Perceptual learning is typically based on past experiences, and every one of us learns to emphasize some information and to ignore others. Experience is the best teacher for such perceptual skills. At the same time, experience creates a narrative. We create mental sets (readiness to receive some information and ignore others) in order to efficiently process the communication that is coming our way. Through the perspective of Urban Trauma, our motives and needs will definitely influence our perception. Lastly, cognitive styles suggest that people will differ in the ways they process and perceive information.

For centuries Blacks in America were told that they were inferior: to create color distinction became the reason, and to reinforce abuse became the way. Now that we understand that perception is created through our experiences and information that we have gathered, it is safe to conclude that over time European's perception of our inferiority would, for some, eventually become the perception of ourselves.

Now in modern times, this perceptual inferiority makes the Black community more vulnerable to Urban Trauma, especially when you are living in poverty, violence, and lacking the adequate resources to excel. The life experiences of Black people through the generations are jaded by past traumatic insults. Those old experiences tend to create a narrative that is a spin-off of the actual situation; creating a by-product called perceptual error. As a result, the outcome or the way you think about yourself or your situation will be faulty because you did not analyze the situation from a clean slate—you have a backstory and that narrative affects the way you finished this one.

Additionally, perceptual errors in Urban Trauma occur when judgments of another's behavior are made using one's own standards and assumptions. So, if Black people use White superiority standards for judging themselves then it is no wonder we struggle with inferiority. Many White folks truly believe that their standards of beauty, intellect, physical stamina, and evolutionary progress are universally held. That misconception interferes with their ability to accept alternative perspectives. When people assume that their way is the right way, then others can only be wrong.

Perceptual errors about Black inferiority are dangerous. Perceptual errors about Black inferiority in Urban Trauma are deadly. Inferiority is the mother of self-hatred. Self-hatred causes you to have little to no regard for yourself, others that look like you, or your community. The rise of Black-on-Black violence is directly linked to inferiority. There are many young Black men that I work with who have predetermined that their life expectancy will not go beyond the age of eighteen. They see no reason to try hard in school or to stay out of trouble when their perception is that prison or death is their ultimate destiny. They think so little of themselves that they do not consider the damage that it causes when they hurt or kill one of their brothers or sisters. Inferiority propels the perceptional misconception that Black lives truly do not matter. This perception is supported and reinforced by White America every day. For this reason, I contend that perceptual errors about who we are (subhuman=error), what we have been able to accomplish as a people (nothing if it weren't for White people=error), and what we have contributed to society (we are a menace to society and do not contribute=error) fuel Urban Trauma at a rate unlike any of the other characteristics.

In severe cases, perceptual errors go beyond Urban Trauma and become perceptional distortions, distorted thinking patterns, or memory gaps/errors.

A Face of Urban Trauma: The Neighborhood Kids

Let's revisit the concept of police brutality and how that may fit into perceptual error. Most recently, I dealt with a case where two young Black teenagers were playing around, goofing off with some friends. There were a few boys and girls in this group and they were doing things that regular teenagers do, like play fighting, mouthing off at each other, getting loud, being sarcastic, and spewing inappropriate jokes. After the group departed, one of the girls noticed that she was missing some money. She called the police to notify them of what had just occurred, stating that she was hanging out with two other boys and that she is not sure who took the money, but the money was gone.

What do you think the police officers did next? They went after the boys as if they were guilty.

What do you think the boys did next? They ran.

How do you think the police approached the boys who were heading back home? You may have guessed: with aggression and culpability. How do you think the boys approached the police? Afraid, defensive, and combative, because they were wrongly accused? Can we explain the police officers' approach, and the reaction of the boys by applying the concept of perceptual error?

Disclaimer: I think that perceptual error is one piece of the puzzle, but it certainly does not explain all of the actions of police officers and in some cases of the allegedly accused. Perceptual error certainly does not completely explain the lethal approach to manage alleged criminality that many times can be managed by using appropriate de-escalation techniques.

In order to bring this point home, review the following chart which uses the framework of perception and then perceptual error. Take note of your conclusion:

Perceptions	Police Officer	Youth #1	Youth #2
Perceptual Learning (past experiences)	Black boys and men are dangerous.	Police will kill me and ask questions later.	Police do not protect they harass people who look like me.
Mental Sets	Black men are violent. We have to meet them with aggression to subdue them.	Police are out to harass the Black community.	Police are not friendly and do not care about us.
Motives and Needs	I need to catch the bad guys.	I need to survive.	I am not going to be disrespected (motive).
Cognitive Styles	These Black kids are probably at fault, so I am going to arrest them.	I don't know what is going to happen (fight or flight setting in).	I am not going to do what they tell me. Police are bullies in blue uniforms.
Perceptual Errors	If these thugs were not out here stealing money, they would not be arrested.	Police kill all Black men.	Police kill all Black men.
Internal Disposition	Wannabe gangsters are wasting my time.	If the police weren't harassing me I would not behave this way.	If the police approached me with respect they would get respect.
External Situational	It is my duty to respond to these accusations and deal with them accordingly.	I have a right under the Fifth Amendment. I am innocent until proven guilty.	I am a citizen just like anyone else. If thing were not so biased then I would cooperate more.
Your Conclusion?			

REJECTION: An Urban Trauma Characteristic

In his book, *Emotional First Aid: Healing Rejection, Guilt, Failure, and Other Everyday Hurts*, Guy Winch talks about rejection and its effects on the mind, body, and soul. In an article published in *Psychology Today* (July 2014), Dr. Winch describes the effects of rejection. Rejection, as it relates to Urban Trauma, is important because many people who experience it have been rejected or abandoned at some point in their lives.

Historically, rejection has occurred on various levels in the Black community. The biggest psychological rejection has come from the White Europeans toward Black people. Many Whites have rejected our race, color, our way of life, the God we worshiped, our family systems, our music, dress, and customs. The sad part about this is that the rejection very quickly turned into exploitation. The psychological wounds have been lasting, for hundreds of years. Some Black people try their best to be accepted by Whites. Others have a simple goal of equal treatment and respect. This type of rejection creates what Dr. Winch's defines as a "psychological injury." The reality is that all people are wired for human contact and connection. As a result, shame and fear around the thought of disconnection is universal.

Here are some clear markers identified by Dr. Winch to increase awareness about the neurobiological impact of rejection.

To deepen your understanding, add "**For those with Urban Trauma….**" at the beginning of each bullet point:

- **Rejection piggybacks on physical pain pathways in the brain.** fMRI studies show that the same areas of the brain become activated when we experience rejection as when we experience physical pain. This is why rejection hurts so much (neurologically speaking). In fact, our brains respond so similarly to rejection and physical pain that...

- **Tylenol reduces the emotional pain rejection elicits.** In a study testing the hypothesis that rejection mimics physical pain, researchers gave some participants acetaminophen (Tylenol) before asking them to recall a painful rejection experience. The people who received Tylenol reported significantly less emotional pain than subjects who took a sugar pill. Psychologists assume that the reason for the strong link between rejection and physical pain is that...

- **Rejection served a vital function in our evolutionary past.** In our hunter/gatherer past, being ostracized from our tribe was akin to a death sentence, as we were unlikely to survive for long alone. Evolutionary psychologists assume the brain developed an early warning system to alert us when we were at risk for ostracism. Because it was so important to get our attention, those who experienced rejection as more painful (i.e., because rejection mimicked physical pain in their brain) gained an evolutionary advantage—they were more likely to correct their behavior and, consequently, were more likely to remain in the tribe. Which probably also explains why...

- **We can relive and re-experience social pain more vividly than we can physical pain.** Try recalling an experience in which you felt significant physical pain and your brain pathways may respond with a, "Meh." In other words, that memory alone might not elicit physical pain. But try reliving a painful rejection, and you will be flooded with many of the same feelings you had at the time. Our brain prioritizes rejection experiences because we are social animals who live in "tribes." This leads to an aspect about rejection we often overlook...

- **Rejection destabilizes our need to belong.** We all have a fundamental need to belong to a group. When we get rejected, this need becomes destabilized and the disconnection we feel adds to our emotional pain. Reconnecting with those who love us, or reaching out to members of groups to who we feel strong affinity and who value and accept us, has been found to soothe emotional pain after a rejection. Feeling alone and disconnected after a rejection, however, has an often-overlooked impact on our behavior...

- **Rejection creates surges of anger and aggression.** In 2001, the Surgeon General issued a report stating that rejection was a greater risk for adolescent violence than drugs, poverty, or gang membership. Countless studies have demonstrated that even mild rejections lead people to take out their aggression on innocent bystanders. School shootings, violence against women, and fired workers going "postal" are other examples of the strong link between rejection and aggression. However, much of that aggression elicited by rejection is also turned inward...

- **Rejections send us on a mission to seek and destroy our self-esteem.** We often respond to romantic rejections by finding fault in ourselves, bemoaning all our inadequacies, kicking ourselves when we're already down, and smacking our self-esteem into a pulp. Most romantic rejections are a matter of poor fit and a lack of chemistry, incompatible lifestyles, wanting different things at different times, or other such issues of mutual dynamics. Blaming ourselves and attacking our self-worth only deepens the emotional pain we feel and makes it harder for us to recover emotionally. But before you rush to blame yourself for…blaming yourself, keep in mind the fact that…

- **Rejection temporarily lowers our IQ.** Being asked to recall a recent rejection experience and relive the experience was enough to cause people to score significantly lower on subsequent IQ tests, tests of short-term memory, and tests of decision-making. Indeed, when we are reeling from a painful rejection, thinking clearly is just not that easy. This explains why…

- **Rejection does not respond to reason.** Participants were put through an experiment in which they were rejected by strangers. The experiment was rigged—the "strangers" were confederates of the researchers. Surprisingly, though, even being told that the strangers who had rejected them did not actually reject them did little to ease the emotional pain participants felt. Even being told that the strangers belonged to a group they despised such as the KKK did little to soothe people's hurt feelings.

As a person who has experienced Urban Trauma, I feel rejected when I feel I am not good enough, I have done something wrong, or I am bad. This is directly connected to my relationship with my father.

Here is my rejection narrative. "I am not good enough" triggers the feeling of rejection whether the person is actually rejecting me or not. I remember when I first got married, I had fantasized to myself that my husband would be my rescuer, my knight in shining armor. All those years that I spent suffering and in pain during childhood, never really knowing the true love of a father, never understanding what it felt like to have a dad that nurtured me, and held me, comforted me, encouraged me. Instead for the time that we were together until my teenage years I felt that my father hated and resented me. I felt so unwanted. I needed the love of a father so badly, yet he would reject me over and over. In addition to the emotional rejection, he was also punitive, distant, and self-absorbed. He didn't know how to love me, and in my innocence, I did not care, I repeatedly sought after him.

That lasted until one day, when we were on the train heading from Queens to Manhattan. I remember he had an urgent appointment, and because I was the family translator, he took me out of school so that I could attend this appointment with him. He woke me up extra early and somehow, I felt special because it was one of the rare times that I spent alone time with him, I did not care or understand the reasons I was really going with him. It didn't matter. I felt special. I had fantasized that he was going to take me for ice cream after our meeting and that we would laugh together. I imagined that he would show me the love I had longed for. It was a going to be a great day. It's important to understand that when Urban Trauma is in play, those who feel rejected often fill in the blanks with expectations. What do I mean by that? I mean that we will disregard the actions of people, no matter how they are acting, and fantasize about what could be, rather than what is. We often do this in spite of having clear evidence that rejection, and subsequent disappointments are looming. We so desperately want to be loved that we hope, delude ourselves, wish, pray, and ultimately believe that the outcome will be different.

When we finally got on the train, it was a long train ride, I was sleepy and started nodding off. At one point, I must have fallen asleep and leaned into his arm for support. That moment was the most comforting moment I have ever had. Until I woke up to him elbowing me in the face to get up and get off of him. He pushed me off with such force. I was only eight years old and my little world was shattered. Rejection didn't happen during all the moments of physical abuse—no, it was at that precise moment on the train. I knew then that he could never love me the way I needed to be loved, and I never tried again to be close or connect with him. At that moment I was not enough and my neuropathways for connection forever changed. The emotional pain I felt at that moment was worse than any beating my father had ever served. In retrospect, I realize that I stopped developing emotionally, and connections became something I feared rather than embraced. I became insecure, and the construct for not being good enough was deeply planted in the recesses of my mind and my self-esteem was subsequently compromised. I continued to grow physically, but emotionally I was stuck at the age of eight, in that very moment.

Developmentally, my emotional maturation for connection and reciprocity in relationships was arrested. On the other hand, what matured were my feelings of anger, resentment, guilt, hate, loneliness and fear—the classic feelings associated with Urban Trauma.

Winch indicated in his writings that, "There are ways to treat the psychological wounds rejection inflicts. It is possible to treat the emotional pain rejection elicits and to prevent the psychological, emotional, cognitive, and relationship fallouts that occur in its aftermath. To do so effectively we must address each of our psychological wounds (i.e., soothe our emotional pain, reduce our anger and aggression, protect our self-esteem, and stabilize our need to belong)."

I work hard every day to temper my Urban Trauma. I also have learned to use some of the lessons from the proverbial battlefield to be vulnerable, compassionate, and loving, to try to help those that live in emotional pain. Today, I approach situations by analyzing all the factors, weighing them, making sure that I remain unscathed (as much as possible) and then I move forward. A little piece of me heals every day.

PART II

Section Two: The Biology of Urban Trauma

Genetics

It is important to understand that many of the characteristics of Urban Trauma do not occur in isolation. Instead, science—more specifically epigenetic research—has now verified that we have been genetically changed by slavery, and that there are serious and debilitating outcomes as a result.

Disclaimer: I am not a geneticist. Therefore, I hope that my review of the literature can make this body of research comprehensible and that I can do this topic justice by keeping the facts as clear as possible.

Let's talk about where our emotional pathways are located in the brain. Our brains have a region called the amygdala, which performs the primary roles of processing memory, emotional reactions, and even threat detection. PTSD, for instance, causes the amygdala to kick into overdrive. Researchers have started to uncover in the last few years, racial oppression has a psychological and multigenerational impact on Black people. Racism leaves a biological and genetic imprint on its victims. What does this mean? Well, research suggests the trauma is embedded in the DNA, our DNA, the DNA of Black people. Trauma can actually change one's genetic makeup and become transferable to subsequent generations. Yes, our genetic makeup, due to years of slavery trauma, Jim Crow trauma, Civil Right trauma, and current day police brutality trauma, plus mass incarceration trauma has changed our genes.

Epigenetic Change

Dr. Farah Lubin, professor in the Department of Neurobiology at the University of Alabama in Birmingham, suggests that "gene sequence changes as you age, and stress can distort that trajectory for the rest of your life." Dr. Lubin indicates that there are different types of stress (e.g., acute, moderate, and chronic). Therefore, if you are exposed to chronic, but also unpredictable stress, your response to the environment can be destabilizing and have long-term effects. Dr. Lubin reports, "epigenetics serves as an interface between your environmental experiences and how your DNA will be interpreted in response to those experiences" (Love, 2016). Further, research conducted by the National Institutes of Health suggests that chronic stress and exposure to stress hormones alters our DNA— not the gene sequence but rather gene expression. To further confirm this hypothesis, more recent studies indicate that stress and trauma can actually change or alter a person's DNA and genetic makeup. This is referred to as epigenetic change. The changed or variated gene is then handed down, genetically, from parents to their children.

The FKBP5 gene plays a role in your body's stress response system a.k.a. the hypothalamic-pituitary-adrenal axis (HPA axis). In PTSD patients, their HPA axis appears overactive. In some of these people, their FKBP5 gene has significant variations. These variations can change how the body reacts to stress. When we are under stress, we produce steroid hormones called glucocorticoids, which affect various bodily systems. Cortisol is the most important human glucocorticoid. Cortisol binds to the glucocorticoid receptor in the cell's cytoplasm and the hormone-receptor complex is then translocated into the nucleus, where it binds to its DNA response element and modulates transcription from a battery of genes. This leads to changes in the cell's phenotype. Past studies have shown that these glucocorticoids alter the genes that control the HPA axis, which includes the hypothalamus and pituitary glands of the brain, and the adrenal glands near the kidneys. Studies involving the descendants of Jewish Holocaust survivors under Nazi Germany found that these individuals had an altered FKBP5 gene, along with PTSD, hypertension, and obesity.

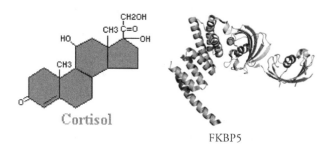

Cortisol

FKBP5

FKBP5

Since research shows that the variated genes are passed down to our children, then that would mean that most Black people have these variated FKBP5 genes, due to the traumas of slavery. From every account, slavery was and still remains one of the greatest atrocities in American history. Recount the trauma that our ancestors suffered. Black people have been subjugated to horrendous trauma for hundreds of years and many generations. Genetic changes stemming from the trauma suffered by African slaves in America are capable of being passed on to their children. This is the clearest sign yet that one person's life experience can affect subsequent generations.

Fight or Flight

I believe there is a direct link to cortisol, the biological fight or flight response, and Urban Trauma. Cortisol is a primary stress hormone, it is your body's main response to stress and it is concentrated in the blood, saliva, or urine. Cortisol, the hormone, typically increases following a stressful event. When encountering high stress environments (e.g., witnessing a murder, being a victim of a robbery, or wrongfully accused), as those dictated by Urban Trauma, emotions such as fear and anxiety are identified. Sensory and emotional information is sent to the hypothalamus, hippocampus, and prefrontal cortex. The process goes like this: Through the hypothalamus activation, corticotrophin and the adrenocorticotropic hormone are released from the anterior pituitary gland thus stimulating cortisol. Cortisol in a high stress environment increases glucose used by the brain and in your bloodstream. It uses only the functions that are necessary for the fight or flight response and makes changes to the immune system, digestive system, and growth processes. All this is biologically happening inside the body of those experiencing Urban Trauma, coupled with vivid memories of past racial abuse and new or recurring situations that are hostile, unsafe, and often deemed threatening.

On the other hand, in low stress environments, cortisol rates drop to normal, heart rate and blood pressure levels decrease to standard levels, and other bodily activities return to regular flows (Mayo Clinic, 2016). It has been supported by the literature that those exposed to and consistently dealing with high stress environments and high levels of cortisol expose themselves to possibilities of anxiety, depression, digestive problems, heart disease, sleep problems, excessive weight, and weakened memory and concentration abilities. Remember, in Urban Trauma, fight or flight is the body's reaction to perceived stress by building up the energy to fight off or flee from the source of actual or perceived "stress."

If we pull all this information together, science tells us that our bodies, under stressful circumstances will activate cortisol, which is biologically meant to be secreted as the body's way to protect us from harm by either fighting back or running away.

Consider what happens to Black people when they find themselves under perceived threat by microaggressions, implicit bias, and outward physical or verbal aggression. It is conceivable to consider that when we encounter these types of situations, cortisol levels, which are already overactive, are further triggered. Now compound the combination of events with historical data about the legacy of slavery and racism, and a "boom" reaction occurs. The body in this type of situation is biologically responding and instantaneously moving into fight or flight. If we understand the science behind this it will be to no surprise that **all the characteristics of Urban Trauma** will manifest themselves in either a fight or flight response. In fact, many researchers have hypothesized that urban communities live in, and with, chronic high levels of cortisol which in theory is behind the leading cause for certain diseases. I believe that the mental and physical health of those with Urban Trauma is consistently under attack.

Epigenetic Programming

As mentioned above, beyond mental illness there are other serious medical implications that affect Black people and are directly tied to the multigenerational effects of slavery. Researcher Dr. Jasienska Grazyna, Assistant Professor at Jagiellonian University in Krakow, Poland, published a 2009 article that introduces the concept of fetal programming. The author suggests that although several generations have passed since the abolition of slavery in America, it has not been enough to obliterate the impact of slavery on the current biological and health condition of the Black population (Grazyna J, Thune, I., & Ellison, P. 2009).

The other bodies of research focus on the genetic impact of slavery on socioeconomic status. One particular study by Dr. Dagmara McGuinness and her colleagues demonstrated that global DNA hypomethylation was associated with the most deprived group of study participants, when compared with more affluent participants. Through her research, Dr. McGuiness begins to make a link between DNA and Socioeconomic Status (SES). In particular, there are potential direct links to poverty and developmental or epigenetic programming in utero; which from the study above we know is linked to slavery. In all, this study presented findings in a group of people characterized by extremes of the socioeconomic status. The data links global DNA methylation status to socioeconomic factors.

Epigenetic Inheritance

Yaa Ama Yancey a researcher from Komfo Anokye Teaching Hospital in Ghana launched a genetic study of 156 Black men and women, plus gathered DNA from their great-great grandparents who were enslaved by Europeans, witnessed or experienced torture under slavery, or were exiled to the South and other regions of the U.S. for personal safety.

Yancey and her research team also analyzed the genes of their children, who are known to have increased likelihood of stress disorders. They compared the results with the descendants of African families who were living in Africa during three centuries of American slavery. Yancey reported, "the gene changes in the children could only be attributed to the trauma of slavery in their great-great grandparents." Her team's work is the clearest example in humans of the transmission of trauma to a child via what is called epigenetic inheritance.

Yancey and her team were specifically interested in one region of a gene associated with the regulation of stress hormones, which is known to be affected by trauma. "It makes sense to look at this gene," said Yancey. "If there's a transmitted effect of trauma, it would be in a stress-related gene that shapes the way we cope with our environment." They found epigenetic tags on the very same part of this gene in both the DNA analysis of slaves and their offspring, the same correlation was not found in any of the control groups and their children (Kinsley, 2017).

Through more genetic analysis, the team ruled out the possibility that the epigenetic changes were a result of trauma that the children had experienced themselves through Jim Crow, segregation, or even the current mass incarceration of Black men, in particular—another serious problem in America. "To our knowledge, this provides the first demonstration of transmission of pre-conception stress effects resulting in epigenetic changes in both the exposed parents and their offspring in humans," said Yancey, whose work was published in *The Imhotep Journal.*

The next frontier uncovering whether people can inherit a memory of trauma? Interestingly, researchers have already shown that certain fears might be inherited through generations, at least in animals.

Uncovering this body of research around genetics has been instructive in connecting the dots for Urban Trauma. Thus far, in the book we have been able to highlight the historical events that have led us to understand that the experience of trauma has never quite ceased for Black people in America. There is clear historical evidence of this from slavery to present-day. We have also been able to identify how a cluster of behavioral manifestations or characteristics are associated to the new and modern definition of Urban Trauma. Several vital and interconnected characteristics exist, such as anger, mistrust, manipulation, fear, perceptual errors, and rejection—together providing evidence for Urban Trauma. Now we have scientific evidence through epigenetic research that our DNA has changed as a result of slavery, and we inherited past trauma at a genetic level from our parents, and their parents before them, eventually passing down those same genetic variates during programming in utero. We also know that these genes can potentially revert after a few generations to their original genetic makeup. However, given the continued insult on Black people in America there has been limited opportunity for gene recovery. We also know that the most affected gene is FKBP5, which plays a role in the body stress response system as does cortisol. These findings support the notion that the aftermath of gene modification and high levels of cortisol (likely as resulted in hyperactive physiological responses of fight or flight) are directly linked to Urban Trauma reactions.

PART II

Section Three: Impact of Urban Trauma on the Black Psyche

The Intersection Between Hope and Despair

There comes a point where it all becomes too much. When we get too tired to fight anymore so we give up. That's when the real work begins. To find hope where there seems to be absolutely none at all.—Grey's Anatomy

After battling a long, exhausting emotional fight, many people experiencing Urban Trauma get tired of struggling. We become weary. Some of us lose the fire that once burned inside to help overcome even the most horrific of circumstance. Some of us are not wired to keep fighting because we have more unassuming personalities. Some of us are on cortisol overdrive and we continue to choose "fight" when we encounter additional stress-induced situations. The battles keep piling up. We are impacted by our ancestors who have fought for generations and feel overwhelmed and fatigued by the idea of the continued fight. Some of us struggle with additional environmental issues, generations of poverty, incarceration, and poor educational opportunities. We find ourselves wondering when this will ever stop, when things will change. It is difficult to imagine a way out.

As a result, there are two outcome paradigms that are born out of the Urban Trauma struggle:

- Hopelessness
- Survival Mode

A very natural outcome of the "struggle" for those experiencing Urban Trauma is to either move into a paralyzing state of hopelessness and despair or to create extraordinary survival mechanisms.

Let's first jump into hopelessness. Many professionals use this word interchangeably as a symptom and an outcome of many psychological disorders. While Urban Trauma does not have symptoms, (instead it has characteristics: anger, mistrust, manipulation, fear, perceptual errors, rejection), it was important to address hopelessness, an inevitable outcome for some experiencing Urban Trauma. For the purposes of understanding where Urban Trauma can lead those who experience it, it was important for me to make a distinction between checking off a box related to "Do I have it, or not have it?" and "This is where it takes me," or "Is this the space that I occupy in my life?" and actually describing the way that it looks and feels.

First, hopelessness (a noun) has been defined as simply "lacking hope," a state of being in despair. On the one hand, to despair (a verb) is "giving up beyond hope or expectation, it is the action of being hopeless." Despair, in my opinion is far worse than hopelessness, because when you are in despair you have given up all hope. For now, I will cover the implication of having, lacking, or losing hope and then entering into a realm of despair.

In their book, *Hope in the Age of Anxiety*, Anthony Scioli and Henry Biller address nine types of hopelessness. Out of all the research in this area, I believe that these nine descriptors truly capture how a person feels when they are in a hopeless state of Urban Trauma.

1. **Alienation** Alienated individuals believe that they are somehow different. Moreover, they feel as if they have been cut loose, no longer deemed worthy of love, care, or support. In turn, the alienated tend to close themselves off, fearing further pain and rejection.

2. **Forsakenness** The word "forsaken" refers to an experience of total abandonment that leaves individuals feeling alone in their time of greatest need.

3. **Uninspired** Feeling uninspired can be especially difficult for members of underprivileged minorities, for whom opportunities for growth and positive role models within the group may be either lacking or undervalued.

4. **Powerlessness** Individuals of every age need to believe that they can author the story of their life. When that need is thwarted, when one feels incapable of navigating one's way toward desired goals, a feeling of powerlessness can set in.

5. **Oppression** Oppression involves the subjugation of a person or group. The word "oppressed" comes from Latin, "to press down." Its synonym, "down-trodden," suggests a sense of being "crushed under" or "flattened."

6. **Limitedness** When the struggle for survival is combined with a sense of failed mastery, individuals feel limited. They experience themselves as deficient, lacking in the right stuff to make it in the world. This form of hopelessness is all too common among the poor as well as

those struggling with severe physical handicaps or crippling learning disabilities.

7. **Doom** Individuals weighed down by this form of despair presume that their life is over, that their death is imminent. The ones most vulnerable to sinking into this particular circle of hell are those diagnosed with a serious, life-threatening illness as well as those who see themselves worn out by age or infirmity. Such individuals feel doomed, trapped in a fog of irreversible decline.

8. **Captivity** Two forms of hopelessness can result from captivity. The first consists of physical or emotional captivity enforced by an individual or a group. Prisoners fall into this category as well as those held captive in a controlling, abusive relationship. We refer to this as other-imprisonment. An equally insidious form of entrapment is self-imprisonment. This occurs when individuals cannot leave a bad relationship because their sense of self will not allow it.

9. **Helplessness** Helpless individuals no longer believe that they can live safely in the world. They feel exposed and vulnerable. Trauma or repeated exposure to uncontrolled stressors can produce an ingrained sense of helplessness. In the words of one trauma survivor, "I was terrified to go anywhere on my own … I felt so defenseless and afraid that I just stopped doing anything.

Let's recap. A possible outcome of Urban Trauma is hopelessness. When you are hopeless you adapt a certain way of feeling and thinking, as outlined by these nine descriptors. Based on these descriptors, you can either become a Catastrophizing Hopeless or Pessimistic Hopeless:

Catastrophizing Hopelessness encompasses an all-or-nothing attitude. Central to catastrophizing is the notion that all hope seems lost and that our situation is far worse than what it really is. When hope is challenged by a new stressful event, reasoning of that event does not consider the good and bad, that both can, and in many cases, will occur at the same time. Instead the mental script is focused purely on the negative. Catastrophizing can happen in two forms, situational with a negative viewpoint ("I am a failure at my job") or future focused with a negative spin ("Nothing ever goes right for me."). When feeling hopeless, these negative thought scripts fuel the catastrophizing event and eventually lead to consuming pessimistic thinking patterns that seldom allow for a positive position to be considered. Hopeless people find it difficult to consider what they can learn from their situation or what they can do differently to change their outcome.

Pessimistic Hopelessness involves having a negative view of self, others, situations, past, present, and future. A cynical lens is the primary mechanism by which situations and people are approached. Pessimistic people are often distrustful of the intentions of others, and suspicious or doubtful that circumstances will actually go their way. There are many reasons why people become pessimistic. Pessimism has roots in insecurity, lack of identity development, discomfort with one's self-concept, and lowered self-esteem. Pessimism is not an act of being realistic, although most pessimistic people lie to themselves in order to justify their behavior by saying they are "being real" or "expressing the truth that others will not speak," or "being transparent, while others are fake." The truth of the matter is that pessimism is the shield that insecure people use to deflect further investigation into their true self, most often because they are not comfortable in their own skin. In my experience, pessimistic people also tend to take on agendas that they do not really own, but find themselves being the mouthpiece for these agendas.

Do you know people who you work with, teach, live around that fit this definition? You should consider if Urban Trauma is playing a role. In fact, look for the characteristics and see which ones are clustered together. For instance, is the person you know angry, distrustful, and/or manipulative? These three characteristics of Urban Trauma combined are a direct fit to Pessimistic Hopelessness.

Based on the descriptors and outcomes of hopelessness, it is not hard to connect how we can very easily move into despair. Within Urban Trauma, to be in despair means that you do not care about much: not about yourself, others, community, or even survival. You have completely given up and are simply existing, certainly not living. Despair at this level may involve passive suicidal thoughts, with associated considerations of what it would feel like to end it all. There is a level of desperation and impatience that accompanies this level of despair—a general feeling of being stuck in life, with no clear indication of how to purposefully move out of your current situation and into a more productive place. The combination of not caring and feeling stuck will sometimes lead people in despair to make irrational and impulsive decisions without thinking through the consequences. Despair in Urban Trauma does not consider life in milestones, instead life in general is considered an unbeatable struggle and obstacles seem insurmountable, the weight of which is intolerable to carry.

It is my opinion that once a person is in this emotional or mental state they will become symptomatic and their mental health and emotional well-being will be compromised, with a strong likelihood of continued deterioration. For those working with this population, try not to justify these behaviors because that enables continued use of these two ways to approach the world, neither of which will help with recovery of past pain, reconciliation with those that have harmed them, or redefinition of who they are and who they want to be. This is when more intense psychotherapy with a culturally competent therapist is more appropriate.

The Face of Urban Trauma: Kelly

The story below illustrates that even simple, everyday hassles and minor stressors for folks with Urban Trauma are rooted in the characteristics and outcomes described in this section. Here's Kelly's story.

After a hard day at work, and subsequently running errands, returning home late, Kelly sits in the car at a yield sign trying to decide which direction to go. Should she go eat (since she was starving), or should she go home and hope that her partner made dinner for not just their children but also for her? Kelly is married with several children.

This scenario doesn't seem that big of a deal. However, if you peel back the layers, this moment is traumatic because at the core, Kelly's feeling of self-worth is in question. Kelly says to herself, "I'm not enough. If I go and get food for myself and walk in and don't offer it to my partner, then I'm not enough; I didn't do enough to make sure that everybody is taken care of or that she is getting what she wants. If I don't get food, I'm still not enough because they didn't think enough of me to actually make sure that I have food or call me to give me a heads up that there was no food for me. It is at that precise moment when I feel worthless." [**Urban Trauma characteristic: Rejection**]

Kelly believed that to take care of her own needs (hunger, in this case) was selfish. "And you know what was sad?" she said. "When I went home and I saw there was no food, I went right back out of the house and went and ate in a fast food place to fill the void. I filled myself with junk. I still didn't fill myself with anything healthy. With weight and what weight does, your choices on food, and how to feed yourself… I become a victim because now my eating habits are not allowing me to shed the weight. I'm holding on to all that pain." The pain that Kelly is referring to is associated with the dysfunction in her relationship with her mother, her partner, her children, and most of all, herself. "The other thing that I'm feeling is that I'm being selfish. I'm being told that I'm being selfish and inconsiderate. And that comes from guilt…I HATE guilt."

Through a process of self-discovery, Kelly came to accept that her fears about herself (the things that are most disappointing about her, the sides of her that are not great or perfect), those things are going to be pointed out, especially by the people who we are close to and know us, and they are there for the world to see. The "ugly sides" of Kelly were discovered, as much as she tries to hide them, everyone sees different pieces of the pain. They're going to be highlighted which then leads to her shame. [**Urban Trauma characteristic: Fear**]

Kelly unearthed her wounds around shame, the shame that comes along when reality hits, that unless she makes an intentional decision to change who she is, she is going to be constantly disappointed. She needs to stop pointing the finger at others, manipulating situations, stop being pessimistic, and stop complaining, stop making excuses and take a hold of her life, because her partner, boss, children are who they are. In the end, Kelly acknowledged that she can't change the people in her life, she only has the power to change herself and how she perceives things. She must change her own actions.

Kelly had a breakthrough. "When I make the choice, it's my decision. I know what I've got to think; I know what I need to do to refill [myself]. If somebody else does it, then it is just *taking* from others versus having the power of being in control of the situation and feeding myself." [**Urban Trauma characteristic: Manipulation**]

As Kelly reflected back to being in that car, she worked on rewriting her narrative. "I really believe that instead of me looking at myself as a villain in that moment, when I came to that yield sign of not wanting to go home, I should have done what was best for me. I could have called and asked if there was dinner. I could have asked if I could pick something up. Instead of feeling sorry for myself and assuming what others are going to do for me, I need to be a hero for myself. I have a tendency to trust what other people say and want to hear what their thoughts are, what their beliefs are, that I lose sight of my own in the process. I should be asking what I think about this? What do I feel about this scenario?" [**Urban Trauma characteristic: Trust**]

Through a great deal of counseling work and coaching, Kelly's journey of awakening to her own truth and learning to value herself will lead to higher self-esteem, less stress in the home, and a resolution to her insecurity and self-doubt.

Survival, not Vulnerability

"I am not what happened to me. I am what I choose to become."
—CARL GUSTAV JUNG

Growing up in Urban Trauma's survival mode usually means that you are trying to get through the day in one piece. When you are in this mode as a preschooler, school-aged child, or even as a teenager, there is not a lot of space for true investment in we, us, family, or community. There is only room for "me." You do not share your feelings, you don't reach out for help, you enclose yourself in an emotional fortress.

Survival mode is very near and dear to me because it is how I operated until adulthood. For me the reality was that the same thing that drove me to create a survival mode to begin with was the very thing that fueled me to survive. See, when you live in stressful situations and you operate from a place of survival, all you think about is a way out, a way to persist, a way to beat the odds. You do not have the luxury to stop and think about why you behave the way you do.

Survival mode: There is no time to develop relationships, to nurture, to co-exist, to share emotions or thoughts, and, most of all, to be vulnerable.

Vulnerability is the antithesis of living in Urban Trauma. Becoming vulnerable means you open yourself up to losing at this game called life. Building a wall to protect your heart, your emotions, and deter anything from hurting you again becomes one of the primary tenets of survival. I, like many others, have learned my way around survival. By now I would most certainly have a doctorate in Survival Tactics if there was one granted by the School of Hard Knocks. Learning your way around survival isolates you. It is hard to consider others in your circle, even those who want to help, or do right by you, because you don't trust; in fact, you cannot trust. Trusting in people is a violation, just as much as vulnerability. Eventually you adapt to living this way. Ultimately, people, relationships, connections, community, and interactions are reduced to mere opportunities for you to be on top.

Here is a story about my own Urban Trauma as told through the eyes of my first boyfriend, Jorge. Jorge and I dated from the time I was about fifteen years old until I went off to college. I truly believe that God knew I needed an angel on Earth, and he decided to send Jorge my way. Even in our young age, Jorge loved me without condition, he tried to nurture me and care for me despite my pain. I was an endless abyss of emotion; nothing could fill my void. The harder that Jorge tried, the more that I found fault in him. If I am being honest with myself, and with my understanding of survival mode, I know that I used him as a scratching post to get my unmet needs fulfilled. I was unable to love the way he deserved to be loved because I had absolutely no love for myself. I had no role model for the love between a man and a woman. I had no understanding of what emotional attachment felt like. Jorge, I hope that I have finally been able to give you a voice, and I am sorry for all the hurt I may have caused you. I hope you understand that all I was able to do was survive, I was not able to love myself, let alone love or be loved by anyone else.

In a recent conversation with Jorge, he recalled a time when we were fifteen or sixteen years old, together in our old neighborhood in Brooklyn. "We were friends and then began dating when we were in high school. You lived with your extended family. That was a messed-up situation. I knew you were going through a lot. What attracted me to you was the ambition that you had. The type of girl that you were. You looked like you had everything all together, even though I realized you didn't. When it came to school, you were very determined, very driven. I felt that I had that in me, but I was very lazy at the time. In a sense, you were inspiring me to do better. Being around you and establishing a friendship... I wanted to be around you. I just wanted to be better. I didn't want to be the kind of kid that just came to school, just hanging out; with no direction in life. You were so driven. 'I want to be that,' I said to myself." [Urban Trauma = Survival mode]

Jorge continued, "It's clear that the one thing that I was so attracted to you for, how driven you were, is the thing that you used against me and 'threw in my face.' I remember when you left [for] college, one day we were having an argument and you said, 'You know, you need to get it together. You don't even know your history.' Essentially, probably because you were being exposed to new experiences in college life, you were saying, 'Step it up,' 'Stop being so lazy.' I will never forget what you said, 'You need to be walking with me, not behind me.' [Urban Trauma = Anger]

"I got angry about that, but then I would reflect. I wondered, 'Was she putting me down?' And then I thought, 'You know what, she's right.' I was hurt; wondering why is she talking to me like this? Is she better than me? Beyond the hurt, I knew there was truth behind it. We were still together, so while internally it motivated me, it also kind of shut me down because I felt like you were belittling me. [Urban Trauma = Mistrust]

"Looking at your family situation, I always felt like you were pretty much on your own. Even though you had a place to stay, a place to live...it's like you were there, but fending for yourself. I think your people cared about you, but they had their own family, and so you were still alone. I know you had to move out shortly after we started dating. I remember that little apartment on Court Street. I think I was too young to realize just how lonely you were. Since you were so driven and so young, I didn't think anything was wrong. You were really good at covering it up. [Urban Trauma = Perceptual Error]

"It's amazing how you think that just being around people would make the loneliness go away, but it doesn't. You can be surrounded by so many people and still be lonely. I didn't realize that what you needed and wanted, was for me to fill a big hole of loneliness you had. We were too young to realize how to be there for each other. [Urban Trauma = Rejection]

"Plus, I think a part of me was a little intimidated. I guess because of my own insecurities and how I felt about myself, as much as I was attracted to you, because of how motivated you were, and I thought you were so smart, I had low self-esteem. The way you were was overshadowing me. I just felt like *oh my God* and I just felt so stupid. But still wanting to be there with you.

"I didn't think you said hurtful things intentionally. Now I realize the whole rejection thing about you; you felt rejected so you would put up a wall. You would sabotage things as a defense mechanism on your part. You knew how I felt about you, but then when you were doing things, to make us fight and argue, I didn't see it as a defense mechanism. I just thought, 'How is she doing things like that?' I just couldn't get it. Then I wondered, 'Am I stupid? What's wrong with me?' I would talk to you and say, 'Don't do this!' But then you would do it again. And I would think, 'This is crazy!' [Urban Trauma = Rejection]

Survival at any cost.

PART III

Section One: Mental Health in the Black Community

A Historical Timeline

1600s	Europeans isolate mentally ill people, segregating them with delinquents and vagrants (even incarcerating them)
1745	South Carolina Colonial Assembly took up the case of Kate, a slave woman, who had been accused of killing a child and determined that she was "out of her senses"
1840s	U.S. reformer Dorothea Dix advocated against the incarceration of the mentally ill in Massachusetts, which caused the establishment of 32 state hospitals over the next 40 years
1851	Dr. Samuel Cartwright: Drapetomania—the name given to enslaved Africans with mental illness Dysaesthesia Aethiopica—the diagnosis of why slaves didn't want to work
1859	Dr. Powell, Superintendent of the Georgia Lunatic Asylum, observed an increase in the number of insane residents
1875	North Carolina General Assembly appropriated $10,000 to build an insane asylum for the Colored

1880	Eastern Asylum for the Colored Insane opened
1885	Virginia established an asylum for the Colored who were insane
1897	Alabama Colored Insane Hospital: 350 patients admitted
1900s	Freud's theory of the Unconscious Mind—consciousness, preconscious, and unconscious*
1900s	Theory is presented that intelligence is marked by racial differences and that Blacks are intellectually inferior to the White cognitive elite
1902	Allport's Social facilitation theory and Pavlovian conditioning—stimulus > response
1911	Maryland penitentiary for the insane Negro is opened
1913	Watson's behaviorism—classical conditioning*
1919	Rusk State Penitentiary in Texas was turned into a hospital for the "Negro insane"
1923	Freud's the Psyche—Id (Instincts), Ego (Reality), and Superego (Morality)*
1936	Piaget's theory of cognitive development*
1940s	Boulder Model clinical psychology programs began research-based training primarily for middle-class men of European American origins*
1946	President Truman signed the National Mental Health Act, NIMH was established by 1949
1948	Skinner's behaviorism—operant conditioning and reinforcement theory*

1950	Jung's theory of libido—psychic energy not just sexual energy*
1955	Festinger's Cognitive Dissonance* Group of African-American prisoners in the Rusk State Penitentiary in Texas rebelled and took over the hospital for five hours
1957	Skinner's language acquisition*
1958	Bowby's attachment theory; Kohlberg's Stages of moral development*
1959	Erikson's theory of psychosocial development*
1960s	Post-Civil Rights era: Institutional racism emerged, which is when decisions were declared and policies were developed on considerations of race for the purpose of creating a power dynamic and control over African Americans—resulting in bias, deficient, and incomplete access to mental health. Oppression included mental health services because of barriers like lack of financial affordability
1960	Vernon Mark, William Sweet, and Frank Ervin suggested that urban violence, which most African Americans perceived as a reaction to oppression, poverty, and state-sponsored economic and physical violence, was actually due to "brain dysfunction," and recommended the use of psychosurgery to prevent outbreaks of violence
1963	Bandura's Social learning theory*
1971	Tajfel's Social Identity Theory*
1973	Vail model introduced to counter the Boulder model elitist thinking by concentrating on social problems and non-middle class populations*

1973	The Health Maintenance Organization Act created treatments for Blacks and other cultural/racial groups; however, access was still scarce
1974	Kolb's Experiential Learning style*
1986	Weiner's Attribution theory*
1990s	Managed care expanded to cover more than 100 million people and included people of color, but the services being provided were designed for European Americans
2000s	Only 54.3% of adult Blacks with mental health issues received treatment, but stigma is still attached to receiving mental health services
1619-Present URBAN TRAUMA	

Created for Whites only.

The History of Mental Health in the Black Community

Mental illness has a dark history in the United States, especially for Black Americans. Many providers, educators, and community advocates may wonder why individuals in the Black community often have such a significant mistrust of psychiatrists, psychologists, mental health providers, institutions, and others who provide mental health. This mistrust did not just appear, and if you are planning to work, live, or interact with people who have Urban Trauma you need to know why. There is a long extensive history of confinement, abuse, and experimentation. In 2002, Vanessa Jackson in her book *In Our Own Voices: African American Stories of Oppression, Survival and Recovery in the Mental Health System* was able to provide a fairly comprehensive chronology of early abuse of

Blacks in the mental health system. History shows us that there have always been challenges for Black people to trust and access mental health care. In 1745, we have our first account of mental illness from an enslaved woman named Kate was accused of killing a child and was later known as being "out of her senses." There is no further discussion about what happened to Kate or how her mental illness was addressed, although one could imagine.

A few years later, according to Jackson, Dr. Benjamin Rush "discovered" a new disease called Negritude; he claimed Negritude afflicted only the "negro slave" and this disease was similar to leprosy. Jackson reports, "The only cure for those diagnosed was to turn White, there is no account of how many individuals were successfully cured from this disease."

The history is sketchy for another century, until another physician identified concern over the mental stability of the negro slave. In 1851, Dr. Samuel Cartwright identified two mental disorders among the slave population: drapetomania, a disease that caused slaves to run away, and dysaesthesia aethiopica, partial insensitivity of the skin often accompanied by lesions on the body. The cure and primary therapeutic intervention to both of these diseases, as recommended by Dr. Cartwright, was whipping. Jackson retorts that it is likely that the cure of whipping was the very same thing that caused both drapetomania and dysaesthesia aethiopica. Go figure! These diseases were clear opportunities to continue the dehumanization of slaves, because while slaves did not have the ability to speak their mind at this time, surely, they would be confused as to why wanting to be free made them mentally ill.

Mental health facilities, hospitals, and jails were in such poor condition that they made things worse for the patients. In March 1875, as a response to these poor conditions and to keep Black patients separated from Whites, the North Carolina General

Assembly created a colored insane asylum for Black individuals who were considered mentally insane or impaired. However, many of the patients were misdiagnosed and were simply placed in these facilities at the will of their owners. In 1895 Dr. T.O. Powell, superintendent, reported an increase in the number of individuals who were insane in the Georgia Lunatic Asylum. He believed that slavery provided Black slaves with the structure needed to prevent them from becoming insane. Can you imagine, slavery was considered a *protective factor* that was eliminated once slaves became free. Powell suggested that the "negro slaves" were unable to have self-control, and for that reason they plunged into all excess and lost self-control. *Are you able to see the connection to the present-day status of mass incarceration and its impact on the Black community?* In the late 1800s those in power did not consider that poverty, disease, war—the conditions that Black people lived in—would be the cause of insanity, the same way today, under the law these same conditions are not considered predicating factors to criminality. Again, the more things change, the more they stay the same. Remember: review, revise, repeat.

The Central Lunatic Asylum was founded in Petersburg, Virginia, in 1870 and established as an asylum for the "colored insane." The hospital was renamed Central State Hospital, and it was the only mental institution for Black patients in Virginia until it was integrated in 1970. Professor King Davis of the University of Texas has uncovered medical records for the majority of Black patients hospitalized in this asylum. Professor Davis reports, "They were admitted because they sassed a police officer, they were admitted because they didn't get along with an employer [slave master], they were admitted because they were on the wrong street." He goes on to explain that the reason for admission was typically not psychiatric in nature, "that was true in 1870, 1970, and 2010," he says, "even to the point that the diagnosis is greater than one could accommodate statistically, so you know that probably it's a false diagnosis."

In the 1900s, the Public Health Service, in partnership with Tuskegee University, utilized Black Americans as unknowing test subjects for syphilis. Though over a century ago, it is a cultural memory that has shaped the lives of Black men. Similarly, the story of Henrietta Lacks also lingers in the cultural memory of Black people. Ms. Lacks, in the 1950s, a thirty-one-year-old woman, had her cervical cells removed from her body and cultivated in a lab without her permission (Skloot, 2011). With both cases, there was no consent, a lack of clarification, and a lack of understanding. Black Americans who were deemed psychiatrically comprised spent many decades in various asylums all over the country being further abused and tormented. Subsequently, in the late nineteenth century, theories around racial differences based on intelligence began to surface. White researchers supported their assumptions based on the discrepancies noted between Blacks and Whites on IQ test and in measurements such as brain size or reaction times. In 1912, Frank Bruner wrote a literature review in the *Psychological Bulletin* indicating "the mental qualities of the Negro as: lacking in filial affection, strong migratory instincts and tendencies; little sense of veneration, integrity or honor; shiftless, indolent, untidy, improvident, extravagant, lazy, lacking in persistence and initiative and unwilling to work continuously at details. Indeed, experience with the Negro in classrooms indicates that it is impossible to get the child to do anything with continued accuracy, and similarly in industrial pursuits, the Negro shows a woeful lack of power of sustained activity and constructive conduct."

Most psychologists, by the mid-1930s supported the theory that environmental and cultural factors affected IQ. Controversy around this topic was initiated by physicist William Shockley in the late 1930s due to his assertion that there may exist genetic reasons that Black people tended to score lower on IQ tests than Whites (Shockley, 1971).

In 1961, Vernon Mark, William Sweet, and Frank Ervin determined that urban violence was not due to traumatic reaction—to poverty, physical violence, oppression, and racism that many Black people endured and witnessed—but instead was a form of brain dysfunction. Instead of the atrocities against Black urban communities being seen as the reason for their psychological state at any given time period in American history, these acts were relegated to criminality, insanity, and pathology. By 1969 Arthur Jensen, an educational psychologist published an article supporting this theory, while suggesting that the educational system has failed due to genetic differences predicated by race (Mark, V. H., Sweet, W. H., & Ervin, F. R., 1967).

A similar debate among academics followed the 1994 publication of *The Bell Curve* by Richard Herrnstein and Charles Murray. This book was controversial, particularly because the authors wrote about racial differences in intelligence, inferring that Whites were more prone to fall under the "cognitive elite" and people of color where not, due to detrimental urban environments and impoverished circumstances. The authors go on to discuss the arguable implications of those differences.

The same way of thinking exists today. Instead of poverty, limited access to education and resources being seen as the reasons for failure to thrive in our communities; Black parents are blamed for inadequate parenting, Black fathers are immediately considered absent, Black mothers are classified as intense or emotional, Black students are penalized harshly for behavioral problems, and Black families are considered dysfunctional. Intuitively you would think that the field of mental health would offer compassion and sensitivity around these topics, given our level of understanding of human behaviors, but the reality is that many clinicians judge as harshly as the lay person. So, what is the alternative for a Black person, when they feel trapped in their situation?

Historically, Black folks have normalized suffering to decrease the pain and hurt attached to it. It was a necessary coping mechanism. During slavery and the years that followed what was the alternative, an insane asylum? Further abuse and experimentation? During slavery, mental illness came as a direct result of the frequent beatings, conditions, families torn apart, rape, or psychological and emotional abuse. We know that there is a genetic link to stress, and what happened to our ancestors is inextricably linked to our biological make up today!

Yet, we survived.

As a result, and due to no other choice, the Black community equates strength with survival and anything commanding assistance, such as mental illness, with weakness (Sue, 1977). Post-slavery, survival was the common foundation that the Black community built itself upon. Relying on others or asking for help placed individuals in situations susceptible to persecution, betrayal, or being taken advantage of. For all these reasons, it is understandable why Black Americans apply negative beliefs, distrust, and stigma to help-seeking. This, in turn, affects our ability to intentionally pursue and achieve mental and emotional wellness. Between the 1970s to the present day, connecting mental illness with weakness birthed forth shame around help-seeking.

Stigma and shame around mental health issues are two of the biggest threats that prevent the Black community from seeking treatment for their troubles.

In fact, it was easier to self-medicate than to seek help for one's emotional pain. Most Black people were and are afraid of being labeled as "crazy," "weird," or different in any way (Thompson, Belize, & Akbar 2004), at this point we just want to be accepted and feel normal. For centuries, the Black community has been focused on physical freedom. It was not until the last few decades that we began evaluating the psychological toll and damage years of continued abuse have had on the Black psyche.

Mental Health Stats for Black Americans

According to the U.S. Department of Health and Human Services Office of Minority Services, Black Americans are 20% more likely to report psychological distress and not seek mental health services when compared to non-Hispanic Whites. Common mental health disorders in the Black community include major depression, Attention Deficit Hyperactivity Disorder, suicide, or Post-Traumatic Stress Disorder (National Alliance on Mental Illness). As indicated previously, mental illness is a conversation that the Black community typically avoids discussing. People would rather suffer in silence than admit that they have an issue or problem that they cannot solve. It is a topic that remains taboo. Many are less inclined to take action because they don't see professional counselors or therapists who look like them talking about these challenges, or even working in those health fields. Only 5.8% of psychologist; 22.7% social workers; and 19.6% counselors—are Black (Bureau of Labor Statistics, 2017). Another hindrance to health care utilization is the fear that mental health care practitioners are not culturally competent enough to connect or understand their issues. Indeed, some patients have reported experiencing racism, feeling judged, and even microaggressions from White therapists (Williams, 2013).

Nevertheless, there is an underlying mistrust of the medical community as a whole that stops those needing support from making strides to get help when needed.

Additionally, disparities and inequality hinders urban communities from achieving health equity. There is data to support misdiagnosing, over diagnosing, or an over reliance on psychotropic medication as the first line of intervention, rather than talking therapy. In addition, many of the interventions that are used in the Black community were not designed or created for Black people. Most evidence-based treatments are tested with White middle class populations and later used with people of color, in hopes that they will work.

PART III

Section Two: Mental Toughness, Resilience, and Grit

The Black community has gone through intense discrimination, oppression, and abuse for many generations, in some people producing a racial trauma experience. Yet, at varying levels of success those with Urban Trauma have found a way to consistently push through adversity and remain resilient. There is a sense of strength and determination that is passed down generationally and fortified as the years go by, and through each iteration of racism and racial hierarchy (Brown & Tylka, 2011). Based upon the Black experience in the United States, systemic racism and racial discrimination remains a common place barrier which creates the conditions for Urban Trauma. Social, economic, political, and emotional barriers bring forth negative psychological and behavioral outcomes for urban communities (Utsey, 1998). Despite poverty, police brutality, and mass incarceration, history shows that those with Urban Trauma have continued to not just stand but persevere. It is with mental toughness, resiliency, grit, and determination that those with Urban Trauma will continue to thrive, grow, and become healthier for future generations.

What needs to change?

For those who have experienced Urban Trauma, it is possible to heal. Encourage those with whom you work, live, and interact with to start with the basics:

- How to build trust again with each other, first and foremost (which includes looking at issues of power, lack of opportunity, and victimization)
- How to find meaning in life apart from the desire for survival
- How to find realistic ways for self-protection and for the protection of family, home, and community
- How to become your brother's keeper, your sister's keeper
- How to deal with feelings of guilt, shame, hopelessness, despair, and doubt

---

A Reflection Exercise

Encourage those living in Urban Trauma to start writing down cultural memories associated with racism, oppression, microaggressions, discrimination, community violence, police brutality, etc. **Bullet points work perfectly:** people, places or things that connect their (a) trauma and (b) racial memories. This will help them filter through and breakdown their truth, while identifying if they truly have experienced Urban Trauma.

Mental Toughness

Mental toughness is typically used in reference to athletes, but I thought it would be so applicable to expand on this theory for Urban Trauma. Mental toughness is mostly a characteristic of elite players and their ability to quickly solve problems, learn from mistakes, and facilitate resiliency. It is created through four strong foundations: commitment, control, confidence, and challenge. Those with mental toughness are committed to the task no matter what. They try to gain control of any setbacks or minor hiccups along the way. They are confident in their ability to conquer the road ahead. It requires looking at challenges and learning to adapt. Mental toughness is about resiliency and confidence. It is a cognitive strength that allows individuals to handle stress productively, control emotions, and commit to the challenge. It is the ability to push through frustrations and conquer the adversities that try to hold one back. It allows for competence in overcoming general and personal problems (Gerber, et al., 2013). Mental toughness is tested when you have Urban Trauma. Those who come out on the other side have not only conquered, but mastered this skill. Mental Toughness is the key foundation that will continue to allow those with Urban Trauma to stay strong in the face of adversity.

The following continues my earlier conversation with Shawn in the chapter that talks about Black men and anger, Urban Trauma, and where he is now in his life.

Shawn's Mental Toughness Story

"Have Black men been emasculated in America? Completely. From the time of slavery until to now, have we tried, have we grown out of that? Or try to make our way through that? Or away from that? Yes. The fact of the matter is that while those things have been historic, that didn't make you cheat on your wife or girlfriend. That history didn't make you shirk your responsibility as a father. I think instead of looking for somebody else to blame for my situation, I see how I could have done something differently.

"Slavery in some ways birthed an intrinsic desire for power and greed that then drove **us** to invite the Europeans in and an aspiration to be like them. White was associated with power and money, and we wanted that, we wanted to be like them. Little did we know that it was going to be the beginning of the end for the Black collective structure and that some of our brothers and sisters were going to suffer and be left behind. But some of us didn't care because we wanted what we wanted. We wanted to bolster ourselves, we started to lose the sense of family and community. Segregation kept us together forcefully, I don't think we realized that the end of segregation would change us so drastically. I see that same behaviors now, between us. Some of us that have made it out of the 'hood look down upon those that are still struggling. They talk down to them and cast judgment and blame, instead of understanding their struggle. All of us Black people are one person removed from being in that situation. Our fate is not guaranteed. Instead of acting like a bunch of crabs in a barrel, we should try to support each other. At the end of the day, my opinion is that as human beings, I think we're just greedy. And, I think there's very few of us who can actually receive enough and realize we have enough. You couple that with America's capitalistic society and economic system where it's 'get all you can, while you can, and f*#k everybody else who can't.' It's the matrix that then just drives us to be at each other's throats."

Shawn goes on to say, "I think that the word, quite simply, is *accountability*. We can blame somebody else for everything that happens to us, or we can stand up and say, 'What are we accountable for and what could we do differently?' I believe that after the '70s, where there was much more of a Black Power movement, then into the '80s, that we just fell asleep. I'm not saying that the '70s was full of well-disciplined soldiers of Black men, but I think there was an understanding that the Black family was going to be the nucleus of whatever we were going to do here in this land, as a people. And then I think that somehow, some way, we just got sidetracked by all the other distractions that were definitely laid in our path on purpose. Those distractions of drugs (from use to the drug selling game) and mass incarceration, were not put there by accident. Every time we tried to focus on rebuilding our communities and strengthen our people there was a new attack on us that we had to deal with. We have to overcome our Urban Trauma and embrace our role as stewards of our families; we need to be there to steer the younger Black boys and men as they are coming up.

"I feel that MY generation is making a difference, but it could just be my personal experience. We allowed ourselves to be pulled astray, by any and everything else; any other distraction. We forgot that our purpose was to basically lead our families into being able to do better than we did. Black men are disassociated from the family because of their own lack of discipline. The Black family is the ROCK of our community. We have to nurture the growth and support young Black couples and their children. Now is the time to tap into to our inner strength, which has been given to us by our ancestors, and become mentally tough.

Uplifting and supporting each other as we try to keep moving the needle toward racial justice. Racial justice is OUR fight. Not anyone else's. We will accept support from our allies but allies cannot be at the forefront of our battle, because they do not know what they are battling for."

By becoming the pillars of our families, providing stability and safety. Teaching and encouraging. We must create a new legacy. That is our charge!

Resiliency

Resiliency is more than surviving. It is the ability to pivot, and move forward from hardships by refusing to succumb to the role of the victim. It is the ability to develop strength (Silliman, 1994), and the ability to return back to a former position without being twisted out of shape (Howard, 1996). Resiliency allows those with Urban Trauma to cope more effectively and emerge impenetrable from the crisis of persistent stress, whether from within or from without. This strength resides in untapped reservoirs of physical, emotional, cognitive, interpersonal, social, and spiritual resources and competencies. It is learning to adapt continuously and trudge ahead. Resiliency is one of the many positive characteristics we inherited during our struggles and can be seen by those who have been through and overcame Urban Trauma.

Kyisha's Resiliency Story

"I have been fortunate enough to go through my journey of healing from my Urban Trauma and really looking at my past, growing up, and the things that happened to me. I came back to work in the inner city, because it's that important. Because these are communities that get forgotten. Only when there's crime, they remember. [People outside these communities] don't remember anything good." A little older, a little wiser, Kyisha has a bachelor and two master's degrees and is working on her PhD. Her journey has brought her to helping other people because now she can.

Kyisha says, "You can't really help others if you're not in a good place yourself. Right? I went through my healing of the trauma, so I don't jump every time I hear a bang (sounding like a gunshot) or get nervous if something breaks. And now I'm helping those same kids that remind me of me. I can relate to everything they're dealing with. I always argue with people, a parent isn't a bad parent, just like a child is not a bad child. People make bad choices. Parents try their best. And how did they learn to parent anyway? From their parents. And if they didn't have parents, or they were absent, where do they learn from? So, they try their best. Do they get it right all the time? Nobody gets it right all the time. But they try, and so instead of going into urban communities (already facing so much exposure to community violence) with the mindset of doing parent engagement, we should be doing parent partnership, number one. [Parents] will be the partners at the table with us. And also partnering with these young people, giving them the skills to make decisions to problem-solve themselves."

Kyisha has turned her experience, which could have otherwise led her to a pretty negative type of lifestyle, into something absolutely positive. She pours everything she's learned and all the skills and education she's acquired, into inner city/urban kids in hopes to change their lives, just the way that her life was changed. She wants to help them realize that they *can* be successful and they could define success any way they want. Recently Kyisha sat with her mother, and her mother asked, "Do you forgive me for all the things I did?" Kyisha answered (compassionately), "Mom, Yes. I told you I forgive you and I love you." She has reconciled that relationship and is well on her way to healing her Urban Trauma.

Grit

I believe grit is the foundation necessary to help urban boys and girls, men and women, achieve success in their future. Grit is defined as the tendency to endure challenging goals with perseverance and passion. Individuals with true grit, work strenuously toward long-term goals despite distractions, failures, and hindrances (Duckworth et al., 2007). For example, academically, many of our urban students are struggling due to distractions at home, living in poor conditions, and not having the proper academic assistance. By using failure as an opportunity to launch into success, those who live in urban communities can be successful with any task set before them (Strayhorn, 2014). Encouraging those with Urban Trauma to apply themselves, apply more effort, and persevere with passion truly has an effect on their performance. Reminding them that success is not solely based upon talent; however, consistency, stamina and effort matters as well (Strayhorn, 2014). People with Urban Trauma who are capable of bouncing back and persevering despite setbacks and barriers are more likely to succeed than those who are easily discouraged.

My group, Integrated Wellness, was invited to assess youth for Connecticut's child protective services and students in an adult education program, all of whom had Urban Trauma. We were asked to measure IQ, personality traits, mental health barriers, and grit. These evaluations were completed to assess readiness for postsecondary options. The results were interesting, in that many of the students—despite their pretty bleak circumstances, (some were living in foster homes, therapeutic residential placements, juvenile facilities, and homes for pregnant girls; while others were couch surfing and homeless)—their grit level remained average to high average. Consequently, while motivation may wane, resources and opportunities scarce, grit remained intact. This project illustrated that kids with Urban Trauma have the desire to do better. Now it is up to us to equip them to actually execute those desires.

Jamal's Grit Story

Let's revisit Jamal. Jamal was able to secure employment, started working as a mentor, and began to stabilize himself. Soon after securing employment, he found an apartment and not too long after that purchased a new car. Over the next year, Jamal got married and is now expecting his first child. Jamal showed grit. He did not give up despite his Urban Trauma. He continues to persevere, even though his homelessness was described as the darkest time in his life. He turned his struggle into triumph and is now paying it forward, by working with inner city adolescent males who also have Urban Trauma. When asked what advice Jamal would give to others in a similar situation, he emphasized, "Don't give up. The easiest thing to do is to give up. **When your back is against the wall, use that wall as leverage to push forward.** I found many resources when I was homeless. People were giving out free haircuts. People were giving out free suits for business interviews and assistance writing a resume. There are options for people out there who have Urban Trauma and are homeless. Don't give up. The cards are stacked against us but with enough pushing and fighting and being resilient we can thrive."

Finding help: Tony's Story

Remember Tony? The one thing that kept Tony from sinking into oblivion and becoming another statistic was his weekly sessions with me. There, he was inspired. He was given hope that he could be something else, that he could overcome his Urban Trauma. He was encouraged to pursue education as the way to a more peaceful, productive, and successful life. He could have family, a community, money to live a nice, safe, calmer environment. Someone believed in him, I believed in him, and talked to him and encouraged him to express himself in healthy ways.

I was the only consistent thing in Tony's life. And Tony started to listen. I was there, year after year, not abandoning him, valuing his thoughts and accepting him, showing him his path by talking to him about our history, his Urban Trauma, and how he can change the course of his life and break the cycle. I was there to support him and give him a positive view of life. He wanted to change his life and had the "mental toughness" to make that work. Tony eventually learned a trade and became a welder and now lives a life away from the source of his Urban Trauma. He has created a new family through friends. His Urban Trauma did not bring him down so far that he could not climb out. He survived and moved forward. Not everyone does. Tony is an example of how the "system" doesn't have to be the end for young children. With patience, understanding, and attention from people who care, success is possible. A "normal" life outside of the urban war zone is possible.

PART III

Section Three: Modern Day Tests to our Resilience

Grit in the Face of Political Whitelash

It is an unfortunate reality that we had to say goodbye to the Obamas in January 2017. The anxiety over bidding farewell was not because they were the first Black presidential family of the United States; not because Obama had the best policies that supported an all-Black agenda; or because his administration's policies eliminated racism and accomplished world peace (all of which was expected, by the way). The anxiety was because on Friday, January 20, 2017, we inaugurated our new reality. Whitelash was happening right before our eyes and we could do nothing to stop it. I, like so many in the Black community, had to wrap my head around why so many intelligent, middle class, White people—especially women—voted for him.

To be clear, for many, this past election was not about the Democratic candidate automatically being the best choice for urban communities. During Democrat Bill Clinton's administration, urban and communities of color did not fare very well either. For example, Clinton's 1994 implementation of the three strikes law. A law which ultimately led to the privatization of prison, an increase in the incarceration of Black men, and the criminalization of substance abuse, which at that time was running rampant in poor urban communities, hit us hard. The distinct difference between Hillary Clinton taking office and the election of Trump had nothing to do with their policies or whether White people would benefit from Clinton as president (because they would have), it was about White superiority. It was a clear message to communities of color that Whites still have the power in the U.S., giving the forty-fifth president the liberty to run a campaign and later lead the country based on racial hatred. From calling Mexicans criminals, to his travel ban, to emphatically stating that Black people live in Hell, Trump's message was clear. How much more racially driven can an election become? How much clearer can a person get about his agenda?

Urban Trauma is implicit in this type of political agenda. In my opinion, Trump's presidency has the power to activate every characteristic of Urban Trauma, and should be considered a catalyst event for those who are on the verge of developing Urban Trauma, or who have not yet witnessed a stressful life event. Many in urban communities are angry, mistrustful, and fearful—all characteristic of Urban Trauma. They see—clear as day—the rejection of their race, culture, religion, and their contributions in America.

I was shocked when I learned that 62% of White women voted for Trump. I guess I expected it from White men, educated or not. Perhaps because White men are keenly aware of the reality that racial mixing will, in fact, lead to the slow annihilation of their race, White women are too. But perhaps I underestimated how many White women felt the same as White men. This election clarified for me that racism is more than alive and well. It took me back to the times of slavery when the dehumanization of Black people was used to justify cruelty. This election and many of its elements emphasized the same ideology of slavery—ruling by fear and intimidation. That 62%, the majority of White women, underscored that they are implicit co-conspirators to the White man's agenda of continued oppression and abuse. Not just of Black people, but of any group that is perceived as a threat to their power. By 2044 Whites are slated to be the minority in America. The diversification of America is inevitable. The fear of White racial inferiority is not an unfounded truth—not almost 500 years ago and certainly not today. While Black people are definitely feeling the effect of years of abuse and trauma, the overwhelming majority continue to strive for better, which speaks to our resiliency, even when face-to-face with a Trump White House.

The Haves & the Have-Nots

Beyond racism, a new division has spawned within the Black community, between the "haves" and the "have-nots." Many Black Americans that have "made it" and have accomplished the American dream of independence, opportunity, education, and wealth have forgotten, and at times, look down upon those who live in poverty and remain oppressed. In spite of our political climate, in order to rebuild, it will take a collective community to survive by supporting, guiding, and strengthening each other along the way. If you are Black and in a position of power, help another Black person who needs your support. Consider the power of the Black dollar and where you spend it. How can you use your money to empower and support Black-owned businesses? My call to action for all Black people is to reevaluate all aspects of how you spend your time, your money, and your resources. What cause will you support that will in turn uplift our collective mission?

The time to make a change is now.

Urban Trauma through a Millennial Lens

There is a new multi-racial, multi-cultural, multi-ethnic, multi-religious generation that is absolutely fearless. This generation is not afraid to take a stand, fight for freedom, march, state their opinions on political issues, and roll their sleeves up to work for racial equity and social justice. I am happy to see that times are changing and that young people of color are more empowered to talk about #blacklivesmatter   #blackgirlmagic   #blackboybrilliance #blackexcellence #blacklove and other affirmations that lift up the Black community. The world is becoming more culturally mixed and subsequently more tolerant of racial differences. Pan-Africanism from all over the globe is surfacing as ethnicities are proclaiming their Blackness with pride. AfroLatinx, AfroCubans, AfroBrazilians, Blasians, Blirish, etc. It's the millennial exaltation of James Brown's, "I'm Black and I am proud!"

Urban youth are being presented with more opportunities to succeed now more than ever before. Many have found a way out of poverty and have broken cycles that have existed for centuries, thereby creating a new reality for their children and setting the stage for a new legacy. There are many in power—Black, White, and anything in between—who are taking action and creating community around urban revitalization efforts. Make sure you are doing it for the right reasons and that your heart is in the right place.

We know that the challenges will continue but there is hope that as each iteration of racism changes, so does our reaction. In fact, we are now starting to anticipate what is coming and can be able to better prepare, plan, and mobilize. For instance, many communities of color, allies, and liberals were not surprised, though they were disappointed when Trump was elected. Many will not be surprised with my prediction that the attack on education is imminent and is the new face of racism.

I believe that the Black community needs to support and empower each other **first**. It is only after we, as Black people, have set our agenda that we can invite our allies to support our work. It is our fight to lead if we are to overcome Urban Trauma and strengthen the backbone of our loving community: the Black family. Perhaps it is time to accept that we were always meant to be warriors ready and willing to continue fighting for our rightful place in this world, all the while taking time to celebrate our unbreakable strength and sheer brilliance.

Afterword

I have known Dr. Akbar for many years. When we met, I knew it was divine intervention, yet a purposeful and intentional connection. We found each other in a place that promoted our learning to become leaders in our communities. Maysa and I have been appointed to do the work of addressing trauma in urban communities; for her as an emotional healer and for me as a political and social activist. Our purpose together is to create a ripple effect in the way knowledge and support is provided in our community, the same community that I serve as a State Representative, a community that is in chronic and continual pain. Dr. Akbar and I have been commissioned to do the work of reuniting the village, not just dealing with the symptoms, but the root cause, Urban Trauma. Our focus has been on community healing, advocating for mental health with those that suffer silently, trying to defuse the pressure that has been on our backs for centuries. Breaking cycles and creating community—that is the vision of our work together. As a Black woman, mother, State Representative, and racial justice activist, I too conceive Urban Trauma to be one of the cornerstones of racism in America. As Dr. Akbar describes it, this trauma is predicated on psychological damage that is ancestral in nature. Notwithstanding, some Black people have been able to break the chains of bondage. They have been able to defy the odds of being disenfranchised and marginalized. They have been able to rise above the generational dehumanization inflicted upon them by society. Nonetheless, the tide has not caused all boats to rise, so as to speak. There are many others who are stuck in a rut with seemingly nowhere to go, and the question remains, why haven't they been able to get themselves together? Well, the truth of the matter is that the impact of trauma on their lives has never been fully recognized, much less reconciled. As a result, a vicious cycle has persisted that stunts their ability to fully engage in this thing we call life. The anguish, fear, confusion, stress, and strain shocks the conscience of the community and the manifestation of the pain erupts in ways that are self-sabotaging and self-sacrificing. Just like Dr. Akbar articulated, the prayer of many of our urban youth was to make it to their eighteenth birthday. Now, their prayer is to complete the eighth grade. We have thirteen-year-olds who are out of control in our streets. They are shooting and killing one another. Unable and unequipped to deal with their brokenness, their minds are altered and ultimately so are their destinies. But it's not just their destinies alone—it's the lives of their loved ones and even their perpetrators that are changed forever. And what hasn't been healed is crying out for help, spilling out into the streets clothed in viciousness. It's crouched in corners and hiding in darkness being stroked and stoked by violence; and shame is the name of the game. It is understood that "what happens in this house, stays in this house." All the while, life is a constant battle to survive in a world that has systematically set Blacks up for failure, but thank God failure is not their only option. There is a silver lining. There is hope beyond their pain and suffering.

It all begins with the acknowledgment that Urban Trauma is real.

As Gandhi said, "Your beliefs become your thoughts, your thoughts become your words, your words become your actions, your actions become your habits, your habits become your values, and your values become your destiny." The characteristics associated with Urban Trauma are survival techniques that can be harnessed for the greater good if honed properly. Imagine how the landscape of urban communities will be transformed for the better—yielding a legacy of healing, hope and heroes that will turn their trauma in triumph! Well, I certainly believe that this can be the case. I believe that we can get back to the basics. I believe that our urban centers can return to being villages filled with families and extended families who love and care for one another with a concern that transcends the fears inflicted upon us by a society that we cannot escape. And I believe that we can turn that fear into a love that trumps hate.

—Robyn A. Porter, Connecticut State Representative, 94th District
Chair, Labor and Public Employees Committee
Appropriations Committee, Member
Judiciary Committee, Member

STAY UP TO DATE

MAYSÆAKBAR

Download the
6 Characteristics of Urban Trauma
Quick Reference Guide at
www.MaysaAkbar.com/UrbanTraumaGuide

RESOURCES

Rapid Access

In my practice we use a treatment modality called Rapid Access. Rapid Access promotes individual and community well-being by providing the most advanced interventions developed for those affected by mental illness, emotional disturbances, and global developmental delays. We use a combination of trauma-informed, restorative, and racial identity promoting clinical strategies. Our culturally competent staff seeks to assist and support urban children, adolescents, and adults exhibiting an array of Urban Trauma vulnerabilities. Rapid Access is a <u>culturally responsive on-call crisis intervention</u> program that is unique in providing:

- Culturally-informed assessment and immediate recommendations
- Trauma-sensitive interventions
- Routine follow-up that includes a summary report, additional case management to the family, school, and community partners as part of a network of providers

Rapid Access, ties the legacy of slavery, generations of racism and oppression, family systems, and current psychological states to create treatment goals. We use these historical factors to connect the dots and inform more adaptive coping skills. We partner with clients and encourage them to explore generational trauma as well as their current

Mental Status (MSE) to make a more culturally-informed decision about their treatment options and community recommendations.

Emotional Emancipation Circles^{SM}

Another resource is one of my favorite programs developed by my dear friend and colleague Enola Aird, Founder and President of Community Healing Network (CHN). CHN's audacious mission is to change the trajectory for Black communities around the world—from surviving to flourishing—by building a global grassroots movement for the emotional emancipation, healing, wellness, and empowerment of Black people. This movement is focused on helping Black people heal from, and overturn, what CHN sees as the root causes of the historical and continuing trauma caused by anti-Black racism: the lies of White superiority and Black inferiority. These lies were first told centuries ago to justify the enslavement of African people and the exploitation of Africa, and they are still with us today at the root of Urban Trauma.

As part of the movement for emotional emancipation, CHN, in collaboration with the Association of Black Psychologists (ABPsi), has developed Emotional Emancipation (EE) Circles^{SM}, a healing process focused on meeting the specific needs of Black people. EE Circles^{SM} are evidence-informed, psychologically sound, and culturally grounded support groups to help Black people heal from the lies, and reclaim our dignity and humanity as people of African ancestry. The EE Circles process is designed to help people of African ancestry overcome key aspects of racial oppression, including powerlessness, exploitation, marginalization, systemic violence, and cultural imperialism.

In EE Circles, participants come together to:

- Share their stories and feelings;

- Deepen their understanding of the impact of historical forces on their emotional lives, relationships, and the well-being of Black communities;
- Free their minds and spirits from the lies of White superiority and Black inferiority, and heal from the historical and continuing trauma of racism;
- Tell themselves a new, liberating, and empowering story about who we are as people of African ancestry;
- Revitalize themselves and their relationships with each other;
- Learn and practice essential emotional wellness skills to help participants be at their best—as individuals and as a people; and
- Develop strategies to extinguish the lies of White superiority and Black inferiority—once and for all.

EE Circles are designed to be facilitated by trained lay people. They are psycho-educational in nature and are not intended to be a substitute for professional counseling, advice, or therapy.

Working together, CHN and ABPsi have trained more than 500 EE Circle facilitators and planted seeds for a global network of EE Circles in more than thirty cities in the United States, and in the United Kingdom and Cuba. In early evaluations, EE Circle participants have reported improvements in every indicator of mental health.

I fully support Enola's work.

Please note that the five aspects of racial oppression that EECs are meant to address are from Speight, S.L. (2007), Internalized Racism: One More Piece of the Puzzle, *The Counseling Psychologist*, 35, 126-134

REFERENCES

Adelman, H.S., & Taylor, L. (2006). School and community collaboration to promote a safe learning environment. State Education Standard. *Journal of the National Association of State Boards of Education*, 7, 38-43.

Adelman, H.S., & Taylor, L. (2006). Mental Health in Schools and Public Health. *Public Health Reports*, 121, 294-298.

Akom, A. A. (2008). Black metropolis and mental life: Beyond the "burden of 'acting white'" toward a third wave of critical racial studies. *Anthropology & Education Quarterly*, *39*(3), 247-265.

Alexander, M. (2012). The New Jim Crow. Ohio St. J. Crim. L., 9, 7.

Alonso, A. A. (2004). Racialized identities and the formation of black gangs in Los Angeles. *Urban Geography*, *25*(7), 658-674.

Atkins M.S., Hoagwood K.E., Kutash K., & Seidman E. (2010). Toward the integration of education and mental health in schools. Administration and Policy in Mental Health.

American Civil Liberties Union. (2017).

Augenblick, J. G., Myers, J. L., & Anderson, A. B. (1997). Equity and adequacy in school funding. *The Future of Children*, 63-78.

Banks, T. L. (1999). Colorism: A darker shade of pale. *UcLa L. Rev.*, *47*, 1705.

Baker, B. D., Sciarra, D. G., & Farrie, D. (2010). Is School Funding Fair? A National Report Card. *Education Law Center.*

Bagenstos, S. R. (2007). Implicit bias, science, and antidiscrimination law. *Harv. L. & Pol'y Rev.*, *1*, 477.

Barbarin, O. A., & Soler, R. E. (1993). Behavioral, emotional, and academic adjustment in a national probability sample of African American children: Effects of age, gender, and family structure. *Journal of Black Psychology*, *19*(4), 423-446.

Bellack, J. P. (2015). Unconscious bias: An obstacle to cultural competence. *Journal of Nursing Education*, *54*(9), S63-S64.

Belle, D. (1990). Poverty and women's mental health. *American psychologist*, *45*(3), 385.

Bennett, D. & Morgan, M. (2006). Getting Off of Black Women's Backs: Love Her or Leave Her Alone.

Bertrand, M., Chugh, D., & Mullainathan, S. (2005). Implicit discrimination. *American Economic Review*, 94-98.

Blumrosen, A. W. (1971). *Black Employment and the Law*. Rutgers University Press.

Boyd, T. M. (2009). Confronting racial disparity: Legislative responses to the school-to-prison pipeline. *Harv. CR-CLL Rev.*, *44*, 571.

Brown, D. L., & Tylka, T. L. (2011). Racial discrimination and resilience in African American young adults: Examining racial socialization as a moderator. Journal of Black Psychology.

Bureau of Labor Statistics (2017).

Busey, C. L. (2014). Examining Race from Within: Black Intraracial Discrimination in Social Studies Curriculum. *Social Studies Research & Practice, 9*(2).

Chafe, William H. *Remembering Jim Crow: African Americans Tell About Life in the Segregated South.* New York: W. W. Norton, 2001.

Chemerinsky, E. (2002). The Segregation and Resegregation of American Public Education: The Court's Role. *NCL Rev., 81,* 1597.

Chemerinsky, E. (2002). Separate and Unequal: American Public Education Today. *Am. UL Rev., 52,* 1461.

Childs, E. (2005). Looking Behind the Stereotypes of the "Angry Black Woman": An Exploration of Black Women's Responses to Interracial Relationships. Gender and Society, 19(4): 544–561

Constantine, M. G. (2007). Racial microaggressions against African American clients in cross-racial counseling relationships. *Journal of Counseling Psychology, 54*(1), 1.

Cooper, H. L. (2015). War on Drugs Policing and Police Brutality. *Substance Use & Misuse, 50*(8-9), 1188–1194. http://doi.org/10.3109/10826084.2015.1007669

Corrigan, P. (2004). How stigma interferes with mental health care. *American psychologist, 59*(7), 614.

Darity, W., & Myers, S. (1983). Changes in Black Family Structure: Implications for Welfare Dependency. *The American Economic Review, 73*(2), 59-64. Retrieved from http://www.jstor.org/stable/1816815

Decker, S. H., & Van Winkle, B. (1994). "Slinging dope": The role of gangs and gang members in drug sales. *Justice Quarterly, 11*(4), 583-604.

DeGruy, J. (2005). Post Traumatic Slave Syndrome –America's Legacy of Enduring Injury and Healing.

Delpit, L. (2006). Other People's Children: Cultural Conflict in the Classroom.

Desilver, D. (2014). Who's poor in America? 50 years into the 'War on Poverty,' a data portrait. *Pew Research Center.*

D.R. Williams and C. Collins, "Racial Residential Segregation: A Fundamental Cause of Racial Disparities in Health," Public Health Reports 116, no. 5 (2001): 404–416.[CrossRef][I SI][Medline]

Dubois, W. E. B. (1899). The Philadelphia Negro. Philadelphia, PA: University of Pennsylvania.

Dubois, W. E. B. (1909). The Negro American Family. Atlanta, GA: University Press.

Duckworth, A. L., Peterson, C., Matthews, M. D., & Kelly, D.R. (2007). Grit: Perseverance and passion for long-term goals. Journal of Personality and Social Psychology.

Dunlap, E., Golub, A., & Johnson, B. D. (2006). The severely-distressed African American family in the crack era: Empowerment is not enough. *Journal of sociology and social welfare, 33*(1), 115.

Dunaway, W. A. (2003). *The African-American family in slavery and emancipation.* Cambridge University Press.

Edwards, F. L., & Thomson, G. B. (2010). The Legal Creation of Raced Space: The Subtle and Ongoing Discrimination Created Through Jim Crow Laws. *Berkeley J. Afr.-Am. L. & Pol'y, 12,* 145.

Elkins, Stanley. (1963). Slavery: A Problem in American Institutional and Intellectual Life. New York: University Library.

Eyerman, R. (2004). Cultural Trauma. *Cultural trauma and collective identity,* 60-111.

Frazier, E. Franklin. (1932). The Negro Family in Chicago. Chicago, IL: University of Chicago.

Fryer, R. G., Heaton, P. S., Levitt, S. D., & Murphy, K. M. (2005). *Measuring the impact of crack cocaine* (No. w11318). National Bureau of Economic Research.

Galster, G. C., & Carr, J. H. (1991). Housing discrimination and urban poverty of African-Americans. *Journal of Housing Research,* 87-123.

Gerber, M., Brand, S., Feldmeth, A. K., Lang, C., Elliot, C., Holsboer-Trachsler, E., & Pühse, U. (2013). Adolescents with high mental toughness adapt better to perceived stress: A longitudinal study with Swiss vocational students. Personality and Individual Differences, 54(7), 808-814.

Gerber, M., Kalak, N., Lemola, S., Clough, P. J., Perry, J. L., Pühse, U. & Brand, S. (2013). Are adolescents with high mental toughness levels more resilient against stress? Stress and Health, 29(2), 164-171.

Gilliam, W., Maupin A., Reyes, C., Accavitti, M., & Shic, F. (2016). Do Early Educator's Implicit Bias Regarding Sex and Race Related to Behavior Expectations and Recommendations of Preschool Expulsions and Suspensions?

Gilmore, K. (2000). Slavery and prison—understanding the connections. Social Justice, 27(3 (81), 195-205.

Goring, D. C. (2005). The history of slave marriage in the United States. J. Marshall L. Rev., 39, 299.

Grazyna J, Thune, I., & Ellison, P. (2009). Fatness at birth predicts adult susceptibility to ovarian suppression: An empirical test of the Predictive Adaptive Response hypothesis. Proceedings of the National Academy of Sciences of the United States of America.

Greeley, A. M., & Sheatsley, P. B. (1971). Attitudes Toward Desegregation.

Guerino, P., Harrison, P., & Sabol, W. (2012). Prisoners in 2010. U.S. Department of Justice, Office of Justice Programs, Bureau of Justice Statistics

Guryan, J. (2004). Desegregation and black dropout rates. *The American Economic Review*, 94(4), 919-943.

Hackett, J. R. (2014). Mental Health in the African American Community and the Impact of Historical Trauma: Systematic Barriers.

Hall, R.E. (1992). Bias among African American regarding skin color: Implications for social work practice. Research on Social Work Practice.

Hallsworth, S., & Brotherton, D. (2011). Urban disorder and gangs: A critique and a warning. *London: Runnymede Trust.*

Hendricks, L., & Wilson, A. (2013). The Impact of Crack Cocaine on Black America. In *National Forum Journal of Counseling and Addiction* (Vol. 2, No. 1).

Herrnstein, R. & Murray, C. (1994). The Bell Curve.

Hildreth, G. J., Boglin, M. L., & Mask, K. (2000). Review of literature on resiliency in black families: Implications for the 21st century. *African American Research Perspectives*, 6(1), 3-2.

Howard, D. E. (1996). Searching for resilience among African-American youth exposed to community violence: Theoretical issues. *Journal of Adolescent Health*, 18(4), 254-262.

Hunter, M. (2007). The persistent problem of colorism: Skin tone, status, and inequality. *Sociology Compass, 1*(1), 237-254.

Hyman, H. H., & Sheatsley, P. B. (1964). Attitudes toward desegregation. *Scientific American, 211,* 16-23.

Ingraham, C. (2014). You really can get pulled over for driving while black, federal statistics show. *The Washington Post.*

Jackson, V. (2002). In Our Own Voices: African American Stories of Oppression, Survival and Recovery in the Mental Health System.

Jargowsky, P. A. (2014). Concentration of poverty in the new millennium. *Washington, DC: The Century Foundation and Rutgers Center for Urban Research and Education.*

Jones, J. (1982). "My Mother Was Much of a Woman": Black Women, Work, and the Family under Slavery. *Feminist Studies, 8*(2), 235-269.

Jones, J. M. (2007). Exposure to chronic community violence: Resilience in African American children. *Journal of Black Psychology, 33*(2), 125-149.

Katz, C. M., Webb, V. J., & Armstrong, T. A. (2003). Fear of gangs: A test of alternative theoretical models. *Justice Quarterly, 20*(1), 95-130.

Kelch-Oliver, K., & Kelch-Oliver, F. F. U. K. Addressing Mental Health Stigma in the African American Community.

Kelley, R. D. (1993). "We are not what we seem": rethinking black working-class opposition in the Jim Crow South. *The Journal of American History*, 75-112.

Kinsley, A. (2017). Study of a Group of African Americans Finds Trauma of Slavery Passed on to Children's Genes. *Grandmother Africa*. Retrieved Mar. 17, 2017 at: http://grandmotherafrica.com/study-group-african-americans-finds-trauma-slavery-passed-childrens-genes/

Kousser, J. M. (2003). Jim Crow Laws. *Dictionary of American History*, 4, 479-480.

Kuo, F. E. (2001). Coping with poverty: Impacts of environment and attention in the inner city. *Environment and behavior*, 33(1), 5-34.

Lane, J. (1998). Crime and Gangs in an Urban Sphere: Constructing the Threat and Fearing the Future. *PhD. dissertation, University of California, Irvine.*

Lane, J., & Meeker, J. W. (2003). Fear of gang crime: A look at three theoretical models. *Law & Society Review*, 37(2), 425-456.

Langton, L. & Durose, M. (2013). Police Behavior during Traffic and Street Stops, 2011. *U.S. Department of Justice, Office of Justice Programs, Bureau of Justice Statistics*

Larson, N. I., Story, M. T., & Nelson, M. C. (2009). Neighborhood environments: disparities in access to healthy foods in the US. *American journal of preventive medicine*, 36(1), 74-81.

Love, D. (2016). Post-Traumatic Slave Syndrome and Intergenerational Trauma: Slavery is Like a Curse Passing Through the DNA of Black People. Retrieved September 19, 2017, from http://atlantablackstar.com/2016/06/05/post-traumatic-slave-syndrome-and-intergenerational-trauma-slavery-is-like-a-curse-passing-through-the-dna-of-black-people/

McGuinness, D. (2012). Socio-economic status is associated with epigenetic differences in the pSoBid cohort. *International Journal of Epidemiology*, Volume 41, Issue 1, 1 February 2012, Pages 151–160.

Mark, V. H., Sweet, W. H., & Ervin, F. R. (1967). Role of brain disease in riots and urban violence. JAMA, 201(11), 895-895.

Mass Incarceration. (2017). Retrieved September 19, 2017, from https://www.aclu.org/issues/mass-incarceration

Mayo Clinic. (2016). Chronic stress puts your health at risk.

McCorkel, J. (2016). Innocence Lost: The Impact of Mass Incarceration on Prisoners' Children and Families.

McMillan, D. W., & Chavis, D. M. (1986). Sense of community: A definition and theory. *Journal of community psychology*, *14*(1), 6-23.

McNeal, L., & Dunbar Jr, C. (2010). In the eyes of the beholder: Urban student perceptions of zero tolerance policy. *Urban Education*, *45*(3), 293-311.

Mims, S., Higginbottom, L., & Reid, O. (2001). Post traumatic slavery disorder. *Retrieved December, 16*.

Morgan M., & Bennett W.D. (2006). Getting Off of Black Women's Back: Love Her or Leave Her Alone. Du Bois Review. 2006;3 (2) :1-18.

Morris, M. W. (2012). Race, Gender, and the" School to Prison Pipeline": Expanding Our Discussion to Include Black Girls.

Murry, V. M., Bynum, M. S., Brody, G. H., Willert, A., & Stephens, D. (2001). African American single mothers and children in context: A review of studies on risk and resilience. *Clinical Child and Family Psychology Review*, *4*(2), 133-155.

Myrdal, Gunnar. (1944). An American Dilemma. New York: Public Affairs Committee.

Nace, T. (2005). *Gangs of America: The rise of corporate power and the disabling of democracy*. Berrett-Koehler Publishers.

Nadal, K. L., Davidoff, K. C., Davis, L. S., Wong, Y., Marshall, D., & McKenzie, V. (2015). A qualitative approach to intersectional microaggressions: Understanding influences of race, ethnicity, gender, sexuality, and religion. *Qualitative Psychology*, *2*(2), 147.

Neighbors, H. W. (1985). Seeking professional help for personal problems: Black American's use of health and mental health services. *Community Mental Health Journal*, *21*(3), 156-166.

New York Civil Liberty Union. (2017). Stop-and-Frisk Data. Annual Stop-and-Frisk Numbers.

Orfield, G. (1993). *The Growth of Segregation in American Schools: Changing Patterns of Separation and Poverty since 1968.*

Orfield, G., & Lee, C. (2005). Why segregation matters: Poverty and educational inequality.

Packard, Jerrold. (2002). *American Nightmare: The History of Jim Crow.* New York: St. Martin's Press.

Phelps, M. S., & Pager, D. (2016). Inequality and Punishment: A Turning Point for Mass Incarceration? Annals of the American Academy of Political and Social Science.

Platt, L. F., & Lenzen, A. L. (2013). Sexual orientation microaggressions and the experience of sexual minorities. *Journal of Homosexuality, 60*(7), 1011-1034.

"Racial Segregation in the American South: Jim Crow Laws." Prejudice in the Modern World Reference Library. Retrieved March 29, 2017 from Encyclopedia.com: http://www.encyclopedia.com/social-sciences/news-wires-white-papers-and-books/racial-segregation-american-south-jim-crow-laws

Raghunath, R. (2009). A Promise the Nation Cannot Keep: What Prevents the Application of the Thirteenth Amendment in Prison. *Wm. & Mary Bill Rts. J., 18*, 395.

Reardon, Sean F.; Yun, John T.; & Orfield, Gary. (2006). Private School Racial Enrollments and Segregation. UCLA: The Civil Rights Project / Proyecto Derechos Civiles.

Reinke W. M., Stormont M., Herman K. C., Puri R., Goel N. (2011). Supporting children's mental health in schools: teacher perceptions of needs, roles, and barriers. School Psychology Quarterly.

Roberts, D. E. (2000). Criminal justice and black families: The collateral damage of over-enforcement. UC Davis L. Rev., 34, 1005.

Roberts, D. (2002). Shattered Bonds: The Color of Child Welfare. Northwestern University's School of Law.
Ross, H. (2008). Exploring Unconscious Bias'. Diversity best Practices.

Reinke, Stormont, Herman, Puri & Goel, (2011).

Ruggles, S. (1994). The origins of African-American family structure. American Sociological Review, 136-151.

Rugh, J. S., & Massey, D. S. (2010). Racial segregation and the American foreclosure crisis. American sociological review, 75(5), 629-651.

Sampson, R. J. (1987). Urban black violence: The effect of male joblessness and family disruption. American journal of Sociology, 93(2), 348-382.

Saporito, S. (2003). Private choices, public consequences: Magnet school choice and segregation by race and poverty. Social problems, 50(2), 181-203.

Scannapieco, M., & Jackson, S. (1996). Kinship care: The African American response to family preservation. Social Work, 41(2), 190-196.

Schmidt, L. M., & O'Reilly, J. T. (2007). Gangs and law enforcement.

Scioli, A. & Biller, H. (2009). Hope in the Age of Anxiety.

Seltzer, R., & Smith, R. C. (1991). Color differences in the Afro-American community and differences they make. Journal of Black Studies.

Shockley, W. (1971). Negro IQ deficit: Failure of a "malicious coincidence" model warrants new research proposals. Review of Educational Research, 41(3), 227-248.

Silliman, B. (1994). Rationale for resilient families concept paper. National Network for Family Resiliency.

Singleton, G., & Linton, C. (2007). Courageous Conversations about Race: A Field Guide for Achieving Equity in Schools.

Skiba, R., & Peterson, R. (1999). The dark side of zero tolerance: Can punishment lead to safe schools?. *The Phi Delta Kappan*, *80*(5), 372-382.

Skiba, R. J., & Knesting, K. (2001). Zero tolerance, zero evidence: An analysis of school disciplinary practice. *New Directions for Student Leadership*, *2001*(92), 17-43.

Skloot, R. (2011). *The immortal life of Henrietta Lacks*. Broadway Books.

Skolnick, J. H. (1990). *Gang organization and migration: Drugs, gangs, and law enforcement.* Office of the Attorney General, California Department of Justice.

Smith, W. A., Hung, M., & Franklin, J. D. (2011). Racial battle fatigue and the miseducation of Black men: Racial microaggressions, societal problems, and environmental stress. *The Journal of Negro Education*, 63-82.

Solorzano, D., Ceja, M., & Yosso, T. (2000). Critical race theory, racial microaggressions, and campus racial climate: The experiences of African American college students. *Journal of Negro Education*, 60-73.

Squires, G. D., & Kubrin, C. E. (2005). Privileged places: Race, uneven development and the geography of opportunity in urban America. *Urban Studies, 42*(1), 47-68.

Stack, C. B. (1975). *All our kin: Strategies for survival in a black community.* Basic Books.

Sue, S. (1977). Community mental health services to minority groups: Some optimism, some pessimism. *American Psychologist, 32*(8), 616.

Strayhorn, T.L. (2014). Making a way to success: Self-authorship and academic achievement of first-year African American students at historically Black colleges. *Journal of College Student Development.*

Sue, D. W., Capodilupo, C. M., & Holder, A. (2008). Racial microaggressions in the life experience of Black Americans. *Professional Psychology: Research and Practice, 39*(3), 329.

Sue, D. W. (Ed.). (2010). *Microaggressions and marginality: Manifestation, dynamics, and impact.* John Wiley & Sons.

Sue, D. W. (2010). *Microaggressions in everyday life: Race, gender, and sexual orientation.* John Wiley & Sons.

Sue, D. W., Capodilupo, C. M., Torino, G. C., Bucceri, J. M., Holder, A., Nadal, K. L., & Esquilin, M. (2007). Racial microaggressions in everyday life: implications for clinical practice. *American psychologist, 62*(4), 271.

Suite, D. H., La Bril, R., Primm, A., & Harrison-Ross, P. (2007). Beyond misdiagnosis, misunderstanding and mistrust: relevance of the historical perspective in the medical and mental health treatment of people of color. *Journal of the National Medical Association, 99*(8), 879.

Taylor, R. J., Ellison, C. G., Chatters, L. M., Levin, J. S., & Lincoln, K. D. (2000). Mental health services in faith communities: The role of clergy in black churches. *Social Work, 45*(1), 73-87.

Tetlock, P. E., Mitchell, G., & Anastasopoulos, L. J. (2013). Detecting and punishing unconscious bias. *The Journal of Legal Studies, 42*(1), 83-110.

Thompson, V. L. S., Bazile, A., & Akbar, M. (2004). African Americans' perceptions of psychotherapy and psychotherapists. *Professional Psychology: Research and Practice, 35*(1), 19.

Tolman, T. L. (2011). The effects of slavery and emancipation on African-American families and family history research. *Crossroads, 3*, 6-17

Udry, J. R., Bauman, K. E., & Chase, C. (1971). Skin color, status, and mate selection. American Journal of Sociology, 76(4), 722-733. Utsey, S. O. (1998). Assessing the stressful effects of racism: A review of instrumentation. Journal of Black Psychology.

Wacquant, L. J., & Wilson, W. J. (1989). The cost of racial and class exclusion in the inner city. *The Annals of the American Academy of Political and Social Science, 501*(1), 8-25.

Wallace, J. M., Jr., Goodkind, S., Wallace, C. M., & Bachman, J. G. (2008). Racial, ethnic, and gender differences in school discipline among U.S. high school students: 1991–2005. Negro Educational Review.

Walsh, F. (2003). Family resilience: A framework for clinical practice. *Family process, 42*(1), 1-18.

Wax, A. L. (2010). Supply Side or Discrimination-Assessing the Role of Unconscious Bias. *Temp. L. Rev., 83*, 877.

Western, B., & Wildeman, C. (2009). The black family and mass incarceration. *The ANNALS of the American Academy of Political and Social Science, 621*(1), 221-242.

Willie Lynch Letter, The. (1712) https://archive.org/details/WillieLynchLetter1712

Willis, T. (2015). And still we rise: Microaggressions and intersectionality in the study abroad experiences of Black women. *Frontiers: Journal of Study Abroad.*

Williams D. & Chiquita, C. (2001). Racial residential segregation: a fundamental cause of racial disparities in health. *Public Health Reports.*

Williams, M. T. (2013). How therapists drive away minority clients. *Psychology Today.*

Wilson, J. Q. (2002). Slavery and the black family. *Public Interest,* (147), 3.

Winch, G. (2013). Emotional First Aid: Healing Rejection, Guilt, Failure, and Other Everyday Hurts.

Woodward,C. V. *The Strange Career of Jim Crow* (New York: Oxford University Press, 1955.

Wright, J. S. (1965). Public School Desegregation: Legal Remedies for De Facto Segregation. *NYUL Rev., 40,* 285.

Wyly, E. K., & Hammel, D. J. (2004). Gentrification, segregation, and discrimination in the American urban system. *Environment and Planning A, 36*(7), 1215-1241.

Yinger, J. (1986). Measuring racial discrimination with fair housing audits: Caught in the act. *The American Economic Review,* 881-893.

Yun, J. T., & Reardon, S. (2005). *Private school racial enrollments and segregation* (pp. 42-58). J. Scott (Ed.). New York: Teachers College Press.

Zenk, S. N., Schulz, A. J., Israel, B. A., James, S. A., Bao, S., & Wilson, M. L. (2005). Neighborhood racial composition, neighborhood poverty, and the spatial accessibility of supermarkets in metropolitan Detroit. *American journal of public health*, *95*(4), 660-667

About the Author

Maysa Akbar, PhD, ABPP, author of *Urban Trauma: A Legacy of Racism*, is the Founder and CEO of the Integrated Wellness Group, a multidisciplinary psychotherapy practice in New Haven, which focuses on at-risk urban children, adults, and families. In addition to her private practice, she is an Assistant Clinical Professor at the Yale School of Medicine, Child Study Center. Dr. Akbar is a graduate of State University of New York at Albany, Florida Agricultural & Mechanical University, and Saint Louis University. She completed both her pre- and post-doctoral training at the Yale Child Study Center. Active in her community, Dr. Akbar serves on the Board of Directors of The Community Foundation for Greater New Haven. A triathlete, she lives in New Haven with her husband and two children.

Photography by Kim Weston
Hair and Makeup by Karaine Holness
Styled by Nathifa Akbar

Dr. Akbar is available for speaking, training, and consulting engagements. Visit MaysaAkbar.com to learn more.